Rebel Rising Within

Janice M. Becker

TABLE OF CONTENTS

This book includes guided reflection and workbook sections throughout.

Dedication

Prologue

To The Woman Going Through It

Introduction

DEDICATION

This book is dedicated first and foremost to my Lord and Savior Jesus Christ. If it wasn't for the strength and wisdom He has bestowed upon me I wouldn't be here today writing my story and speaking to audiences.

To my children. You have been my strength, even on days you didn't realize I needed it. The biggest and greatest accomplishment of my life will always be being your mom.

To my parents, thank you for instilling in me a foundation of faith. My journey to God began the day I became your daughter, and He has carried me through more than I ever thought I could survive. Thank you for being there to support me and cheer me on. Your love and support have been one of the greatest blessings of my life.

To my close family and friends, thank you for being my cheerleaders.

To the women going through something in silence, fighting the greatest battles or simply trying to make it through them, this is for you.

To every woman who has ever gone through a difficult season and showed up even when it felt like she couldn't.

To Betsy Pepine. If it wasn't for your moment of mentoring me, this wouldn't exist. Thank you.

PROLOGUE

For the past three years, I've thought about writing this book. For a long time, I wrestled with it. I kept thinking, "Who am I for anyone to care enough to read about me?" And "I don't have the time." But then I had a conversation with Betsy Pepine, author, mentor, and real estate mogul, and she helped me break open the box I had been keeping all of this in.

This book isn't just sharing my story. It's for every woman who has gone through, or is going through, a difficult season and doesn't know how she can keep going. It's a reminder that there is something in you that knows, that sees, that survives, even when you feel worn down to nothing.

That's why I created a reflection section after almost every chapter. Not to keep the focus on me, but to help you find the Rebel Rising within yourself, the part of you that notices what's not right, stops shrinking, and starts choosing what is healthy.

Some names and identifying details have been changed to protect privacy.

To The Woman Going Through It

I see you.

I feel you.

I am you.

Let's Rise!

Rebel Rising Within

Introduction

I was thirty-seven years old, fighting for my life while trying to reach 911.

My children were asleep in the house. My body was broken and bloodied. Every bone screamed. Every breath was a shard of glass.

Looking up at the sky and praying so hard, all I could think was God, please let me survive this.

My assailant kept pacing back and forth. The man who claimed to love me walked toward his truck to get his gun.

That night should have ended my story. It didn't.

But this book is not about one night.

It is about surviving over and over again.

Long before that moment, I had already learned what it meant to grow up too fast. I became a mother at sixteen. I navigated marriage, divorce, rebuilding, and starting again, more than once. I learned how to carry responsibility early, how to keep moving when life demanded more than felt fair, and how to stand up even when I was exhausted.

The assault was not the beginning of my strength.
 It was the moment that revealed how much strength had already been built.

Today, the woman who walks into boardrooms and high-stakes meetings is a respected entrepreneur, a business leader, and someone who refuses to be silenced. But that confidence was earned through years of hard decisions, painful endings, and choosing myself when it would have been easier not to.

I am not a cautionary tale.
I am a blueprint.

My story includes the labels society often uses to limit women: teen mother, twice divorced, survivor of violence. But those labels never tell the whole story. For every setback, there was a resolve. For every loss, a rebuilding. I never surrendered my voice, even when it was tested.

This is not a book about recovery. It is about reclamation.

It is about learning to trust yourself again.
To recognize red flags.
To walk away when something is no longer healthy.
And to build a life that aligns with who you are becoming, personally and professionally.

This is the story of my Rebel Rising.

I wrote this book for women who have survived more than one version of loss. For those who have rebuilt quietly. For those who have questioned their strength, their instincts, or their worth.

Inside these pages, I walk you through the choices, the battles, and the turning points that shaped me, and invite you to reflect on your own.

You will see how:

- ♦ Grace helped me release what I could not control.

- ♦ Grit drove me to build a career in a cutthroat industry.

- ♦ Tenacity carried me through the most extreme personal and professional battles I would ever face.

When you finish this book, you will be able to see your own story differently, not as baggage, but as proof.

This memoir is your beginning.

What you choose next is where your Rebel Rising begins.

Chapter 1

The Night That Changed My Life

I don't think many people are able to identify the single night that would change the trajectory of their entire life. I've had many moments that have changed the direction of my life, but there is one, above all, that changed everything. That night wasn't just my first taste of teenage chaos; it was the moment the ground gave way, forcing me to build a foundation out of nothing but shame and silence.

The year was 1998, and I had just transferred to a new school for my freshmen year. The biggest concern was who to sit with in art class. That's where it started: two boys laughing. One, with spiky brown hair, asked me to the Homecoming dance. I thought his friend was cuter, but I said yes. That single choice would change the course of my life.

The night of the dance, my date Ryan came to my house with his cute friend Damon and Damon's date.

They brought a bouquet of roses for each of us. We took pictures with our dates. My mom had spoken to my dates mother, and I had permission to stay over at his house after the dance. Everything seemed fine.

The dance ended, and we went back to Ryan's house to change our clothes. That's when I saw the setup was a lie. His mom wasn't home; she was at work. His dad was drunk and passed out on the couch.

Ryan's uncle handed him the keys to his car, even though he was too young and didn't have a license. He told us we were going to a bonfire. I had no idea what that even was. I had never been to one.

When we showed up, the parents hosting the bonfire told us to turn over the keys because some kids were drinking. We said we weren't going to, but they still took them.

I was instantly terrified. I had no idea where I was, and now we were stranded. I didn't know anyone there. Damon, the cute friend, turned out to be a jerk, and his date wasn't nice to me either. I followed them to the fire.

As I looked across the yard, I saw him, a tall, handsome blonde guy in a letterman jacket with the bluest eyes I had ever seen. I was mesmerized. There was something about him, something that drew me in like a strong, magnetic pull.

We decided the party wasn't fun and found a way to get our keys back. The boys ran into a friend of theirs from school who needed a ride, so they brought him back to the house with us.

They pulled out a bottle of Goldschlager. I'd never heard of it. It was cinnamon schnapps with little gold flakes floating inside the bottle. It looked pretty, so I tried a sip. It was disgusting. The guys loved it, though, and kept drinking. The other girl was leaving, going home. I thought about calling my parents, but it was after 1 AM and I didn't want to wake them up. My dad had to work early.

The guys eventually passed out: Ryan in the recliner, Damon on the pull-out sofa, and the new guy downstairs. Not knowing where to sleep, I lay down next to Damon.

I had just started to fall asleep when I was woken up by a hand down my pants. I opened my eyes. It was the kid we had picked up.

I was horrified. I yelled, "What the fuck are you doing? Go downstairs right now!" I woke Ryan, but he was so drunk he didn't understand or care what I was saying. I went back to bed, crying and shaken. Damon put his arm around me, and I finally fell back to sleep.

When Monday came, the labels started flying, but they were about the wrong thing. My date went around school telling everybody that I had willingly messed with that boy. They called me names over a lie, while I was silently carrying a secret that was ten times heavier.

Bullying and taunting were immediate, in every classroom. Even my own cousin joined in. The boys called me on the phone later that day, and Damon was saying the nastiest, most untrue things.

I couldn't believe how cruel they were. Instead of holding him accountable, they were destroying my reputation when I was still the new girl. The humiliation was so bad I dropped out of art class just to escape it.

I couldn't stop thinking about the blonde-haired boy with the sharp blue eyes. A few days later in history class, I befriended a girl who had gone to school for a long time.

I told her about the very cute blonde guy from the bonfire. She asked me what he looked like, and when I described him,

she said, "I think I know exactly who you
are talking about."

Reflection
Honoring the Inner Voice

Your journey shows how the secrets we keep are often the heaviest burdens we carry. Before you can unleash the Rebel, you must acknowledge the wounds that created the silence.

A Note to You

When you name the silence, you take back its power.

Rebel Rising

Take your time with this on the next page.

What is the earliest moment you remember choosing silence over truth? What were you protecting yourself from?

Chapter 2

High School Sweethearts Gone Wrong

I fell fast and hard for Josh and looking back, I get why now. He wasn't just a cute blonde boy; he was a wall. I needed him to protect me from the noise, shame, and trauma. I couldn't speak out loud. He became my first, fragile attempt to create a safe place in a world that had suddenly become very dangerous.

We connected immediately. We shared the same initials, both were blonde with blue eyes, tall, same interests in music and movies. We quickly became one of the school's most popular couples, but that didn't stop the bullying.

One day at lunch, my former date and his cute friend were running their mouths about me, and Josh wasn't having any of it. He put them in their place quickly and not much was ever said to me again.

Josh and I started spending a lot of time together, whether it was after school or going on shopping trips with his mom. We were together more than we were apart. Christmas came and went and then came New Year's. My parents agreed to let me stay there on

The condition that his mom was there. She was, until she had to leave for work that morning, and that's when it happened. Our intimacy grew into the physical kind that early morning, and nothing would ever be the same again.

For a while things were okay, but then he started to become aggressive. Call it teenage hormones, maybe? We would get into screaming matches, sometimes over the silliest of things, and sometimes over things that deeply hurt me, that he just couldn't seem to understand. Like when I found his playboy magazines and wanted to go home, and then when we were nearly to my house, we made up and he turned around to take me back to his house for a while. It became toxic, but back then we didn't really know what that meant. One day it became physical. I can't remember exactly what prompted it. I just remember being on his bed and him sitting on my rib cage. He was a lot bigger than I was. I was a tiny little thing, five foot eight and about one hundred ten pounds, while he was well over six feet and around one hundred eighty pounds. My ribs were bruised from that incident, and my parents no longer permitted me to see him. So that was that, or so you'd think. But was it?

Reflection
Redefining Safety and Power

When the world feels unsafe, we often build shelters out of people instead of the truth. But what happens when those walls start to close in? True safety isn't found in someone else's protection; it's built when you learn to trust your own strength.

A Note to You

You didn't build that wall for nothing. You built it to survive. Today, you must decide what still belongs.

Rebel Rising

Take your time with this on the next page.

Think of a time you attached yourself to someone, something, or a role because it felt safe.

What were you protecting yourself from?

Chapter 3

The Summer That Shaped Me

That summer my parents decided that my mom, brother and I would go to Ocean City, MD, where my grandmother owned a motel called the Ocean Lodge, and would stay the entire summer to help her.

This gave me the opportunity to have my own private room with a roommate, my grandma's employee, Brandy, whom I met the summer before and really hit it off with. They surprised me with her by having her hide in the motel laundry room. It was one of the happiest moments of my summer.

I would help my grandma with the front desk, answer the phone, make reservations, and clean rooms. As the summer went on, I also got a job waitressing at a little Greek diner across the street called Dina's and began babysitting for a customer when I wasn't working the two other jobs.

My time in Ocean City was a huge part of my life. It taught me work ethic, what it was like to be an entrepreneur and a businesswoman as I watched my grandma in action. They are the best memories of my life, and I look back on that time now so grateful for every experience and every person I met.

I'll never forget one evening I was sitting out on the porch of the motel, as I often did, watching the traffic drive by, the people walking across the street, and the sounds and smells that filled the air. A former employee of my grandma's, who was also a seasonal renter of hers, came down and we began to talk. I can't remember his name, but I remember he was a bit older than me, incredibly handsome and had a girlfriend that we all were wondering about, because she was not very nice and not very attractive.

As we sat talking, I may have been flirting a little bit. He was asking how summer was going and I was telling him about everything I had been doing. He asked what my plans were going to be after I graduated high school since I was going into my sophomore year. I told him I really wanted to go to college and be a businesswoman. I said to him "Everyone in my town ends up pregnant as a teenager or on drugs", and I didn't want that for my life. Little did I know how those words would later haunt me.

I was really missing Josh during this, and this was the 90's. We didn't have cellphones like we did today. So, I purchased a prepaid calling card, because we couldn't call long distance from our room. I remember calling him and the spark was still there. He wanted to see me when I got back. I told him I didn't know how that would work, since my parents were still really upset over what he had done to me, but I knew I would see him at school at least.

Summer had come to an end, and I was excited to get home to my dogs and my stuff. I was also excited that I had earned enough money to buy my own school clothes and could get basically anything I wanted, whereas we usually didn't have much money at all for me to go shopping on. I loved having money and couldn't wait to show up to school looking super cute in my new clothes and my new platform Skechers.

That summer did more than give me a tan and spending money; it showed me what it felt like to depend on myself. Watching my grandma run the motel, I saw what it meant to be a woman in charge, handling everything from guests, difficult employees, to payroll, like it was second nature.

I didn't know it then, but I was watching the kind of strength I'd later need in my own life. It was the first time I understood that independence could feel like freedom, and freedom could feel like peace, and I loved that feeling.

Reflection
Awakening the Independent Spirit

The Rebel doesn't always show up with fire; sometimes she whispers through small victories. The moment you realize you can create your own safety instead of waiting for someone to offer it.

A Note to You

Every act of independence is a declaration of worth. The more you trust yourself to create your own life, the less you'll need permission to live it.

Rebel Rising

Take your time with this on the next page.

Where do you see your independence showing up in your story? What moment reminds you, you're stronger than you think?

Chapter 4

The Prophecy Comes to Fruition

Josh quickly found me when we returned to school. He was cuter than ever, and I knew I had to figure out how we could get back together, with my parents' blessings. I was assigned to study hall that year and quickly became friends with a girl that sat next to me.

Her name was Jennifer. It turned out that Jennifer was cousins with Josh and lived just one block away from him. I started going over to Jennifer's house and this allowed me the chance to see Josh from time to time.

On Christmas eve of 1999, he came over to her house with a bouquet of roses, told me how much he loved me and stayed the night with me. The next morning, he left and told me he was in love with someone else. I was incredibly hurt and beyond angry. I couldn't believe he would do that to me. Worst yet, I couldn't even share it with my mom and had to act happy on Christmas when I was so hurt.

A few weeks had gone by, and we hadn't spoken once. I would deliberately go different ways at school so I wouldn't see him.

One day I was cleaning my room and looked up at my calendar and noticed that I hadn't gotten my period. This couldn't happen to me. I sat down with that calendar and went through it. I must have looked back through it a few times, counting the days; my heart began to race, the room began to spin, and sure enough, I realized I was late!

Not knowing what to do, I called my best friend, Gabby. I told her I needed to take a pregnancy test and there was absolutely no way I was going to tell my mom. They had no clue that I had seen Josh and being that I was forbidden to see him, I did not want to explain what had happened.

We tried going to the local clinic, but they wouldn't give me a test without my parents or legal guardian, so that was a bust. My friends had the bright idea of stealing me one, because we had no money.

I'll never forget my friend Bryan going and stealing it for me, I walked right into the store bathroom he took it from to take it, and I was so nervous, I dropped it in the toilet. So, he went and stole another one for me.

He handed it to me as I sat waiting in my car and said, "This time, don't drop it in the toilet." I decided to drive over to the mall to take it in one of the store bathrooms instead. It took less than three seconds, and it showed two lines. My heart sank. I was on birth control. How could this happen? My parents are going to kill me. The words I'd spoken just a few months earlier came rushing back. My thoughts raced. What was I going to do?

Gabby and I spent that night at a friends house. I couldn't sleep most of that night. I couldn't believe this was my reality. I was terrified in so many ways. I didn't know how I was going to tell my parents.

I decided to keep it quiet for as long as I could. I was still reeling from the shock, and I knew that my parents would kill me once they found out. Especially my dad. I didn't want to hurt, upset or disappoint my dad.

I tried faking my period. I knew my mom would notice I hadn't used any of my usual feminine hygiene products. So, occasionally I would throw a few empty wrappers in the garbage.

Somehow, she still knew it.

One day my mom confronted me. She asked me to sit down on the couch and just asked me flat out. I began to sob into my hands. She gently consoled me, and rubbed my back, then quietly asked, "Who's is it? You aren't seeing anyone."

I told her "Josh." She was in shock and of course had a lot of questions. She knew how mad my dad would be and didn't want to get him upset until we knew without a doubt, I was pregnant and scheduled me for an appointment. The doctor confirmed I was 11 weeks pregnant and let us hear the heartbeat. My mom was in tears at the sound of her grand baby. It still didn't seem real to me.

The doctor told me that if I decided I wanted to terminate my pregnancy, there was still time. I remember being so upset by that, I demanded that she find me another doctor. I was not going to terminate my baby, but now we had to figure out how to break the news to my dad.

We decided I would go stay with my friend Gabby at her dad's place, since my dad didn't know where it was. My mom had my aunt, my dad's sister, come over so she could tell him the news. Just as we expected, it didn't go well. I mean, who could blame him? No father wants to hear that his teenage daughter is pregnant.

I spent three days at my friend's house before my mom told me it was safe for me to come home. The look of disappointment on my dad's face is one that has never left me. He said some things, things I know my dad didn't believe in his heart but said out of anger, and I can't blame him. One of them was "Your future is over. You've just ruined your life."

The moment those words left my father's mouth, something inside me changed. It sparked a determination in me that I didn't know could exist. I had made a mistake, yes, but I wasn't ruined.

For the first time, I saw how other people's fears could shape my future if I let them. That was the beginning of my rebellion; the quiet promise I made to myself that I would prove them wrong, not out of spite, but out of purpose.

I didn't know how it was going to work out, but I knew I loved this baby more than anything, and I would figure it all out.

Reflection
Turning Judgment into Fuel

The world and the people in it will always have opinions about who you are and what you're capable of. Sometimes those opinions echo louder than your own voice. But every time you refuse to accept someone else's definition of you, you reclaim a piece of your power.

A Note to You

Every time someone underestimates you, they hand you a match. You decide whether to light the flame or blow it out.

Rebel Rising

Take your time with this on the next page.

What words or judgments from others have tried to define your worth or your future? How have you used that pain as motivation, or how could you begin to now?

Chapter 5

Congratulations It's a Boy!

My mom called Josh's mom, and we all got together to talk about the news and how to move forward. Josh felt he had to be with me; it was the 'right thing' to do, and we still cared for each other deeply, despite his current girlfriend. He broke it off with her, and just like that, we were a couple again.

I started showing around springtime. I had a series of medical tests because of the medication I'd been on, which we later found out was the reason why my birth control had failed.

Josh went with me to Lamaze classes. At school, I joined a program for pregnant moms led by a sweet woman I'll call Mrs. K, who made sure I had the education to be prepared. As the school year ended, my support system scattered.

My mom and brother once again went down to Ocean City to help my grandma, but I had to stay behind because of my condition. My dad worked constantly, so the plan was for me to stay with Josh and his mom at times.

This arrangement was great at first. I bonded with Josh's mom, and I got a glimpse of what our future could look like, a kind of play-acting at being married and living together.

But Josh was still a teenage boy, and the reality of my pregnancy was a problem he was not mature enough to face.

While I was seven months pregnant and confined to the couch, he was still living his carefree life. He would go out with friends and leave me alone for hours. He'd get angry and argue with me over the silliest things, like when he felt I had insulted his car.

Instead of having the loving care and support I needed as I got further along, I felt increasingly isolated. The silence in his house was deafening. The future I thought we were building was clearly only visible to me.

One day, he called and told me he didn't want to be with me anymore. I was seven months pregnant.

My parents debated when Mom should come home. My Grandma hoped she could stay until the end of the season, but with Josh gone, I only had my dad when he wasn't at work. Mom came home in early August. My due date was mid-September, but my son had other plans. He arrived six weeks early, weighing six pounds, one and a half ounces, on what would have been my first day of junior year.

I was in labor for almost an entire day. No one had truly prepared me for what was going to happen. I had never heard of an episiotomy or been told that some babies must be vacuumed out, giving my son a temporary cone head.

Josh and his mom came to the hospital, and he was with me most of the time. After my son was born, Josh and I got back together, but it was short-lived. That following spring, a few days before prom, we broke up for the final time.

I was very blessed to have the support of my parents, but that arrangement created its own set of challenges. My mom became a pseudo-mom to my son while I was in school and working. It made me feel like I didn't always have the control most mothers have.

I was working two jobs at a couple of convenience stores. My school had a work program for seniors, so I would leave school at 11:00 AM every day and head straight to work. I wasn't really thinking about a future career or college anymore. I was purely surviving and I really wanted to have my own car.

One day, my mom received a call from a woman offering a demonstration of their new vacuum in exchange for a free case of soda. My mom agreed, and the woman came over. She was polished, well-spoken, and incredibly encouraging.

She started telling us how she and her husband owned a franchise and how passionate she was about sales and marketing, a phrase I'd never heard before.

My mom asked her to tell us more. I'll never forget my mom looking over at me and saying, "Janice, that really sounds perfect for you."

My third job was working for that company. It was a rigorous but valuable introduction to the world of sales and marketing. Our primary job was going door to door and conducting surveys that served as lead qualifiers. Some people were kind, while others were very mean, but it taught me two immediate lessons: how to speak to anyone and how to handle rejection. When I performed the vacuum demonstrations, it also taught me the power of persuasion and language.

It was an extremely challenging, grueling job, selling a $2,000 vacuum in 2001, right after 9/11. After a few months, I quit that sales job and one of my cashier jobs so I could focus on just one.

Before I knew it, it was high school graduation.

I was excited, nervous, and simply ready to be done. I was already managing adulthood, and the people around me, while they were my age, weren't on the same wavelength. I never felt like I truly belonged anymore.

When they called my name, I walked across that stage and looked up into the stands. My parents were there. My son was there. Seeing them waiting for me was the moment I felt truly accomplished. Statistically, I was. In the early 2000s, less than half of teenage mothers earned a high school diploma. I beat the odds.

My son was photographed with me in my cap and gown, and that photo was featured in the high school yearbook.

For some, they may have thought he was my baby brother and had no idea what a proud moment that truly was for me.

That diploma was not just a piece of paper; it was my proof that I was not a statistic. It was also proof to myself and to my parents, that all because I was a teen mom, that didn't limit me.

Reflection

When Survival Became Strength

There are seasons where the world decides who you are before you ever get a chance to. People have opinions, expectations, and judgments, and if you're not careful, they start speaking louder than your own voice. You don't have to prove anything to anyone.

A Note to You

Being underestimated doesn't get the final word. It's just the moment you decide what you're going to do with it.

Rebel Rising

Take your time with this on the next page.

What did that season prove to you about your strength, even if you didn't have the words for it then?

Chapter 6

Welcome To Adulthood

While I had already gotten a bigger taste of adulthood than most teenagers, the summer after graduation really put things in perspective for me. I was working full-time as a cashier and deli clerk, and it was becoming very clear that I wanted more for my life than that. I'm not saying there's anything wrong with having that as your full-time job. What I'm saying is, I always felt called to something different.

I've always believed that when something isn't meant for us, God will make us so uncomfortable in that place or situation that we're literally forced out of it. That's exactly what happened to me.

One day, I came back to work after taking a day off for a severe migraine, only to be met by my boss's wife, who was furious with me for missing a shift.

She chewed me out and told me that if it happened again, I'd be terminated. The next morning, I handed in my two weeks' notice. I wasn't going to tolerate

 Working for someone who couldn't show me an ounce of sympathy. I didn't know what I was going to do next, but I knew I would find something else.

The year was 2002, and the internet, and how we used it, was still new. Back then, if you were looking for a job, you didn't scroll through listings online; you opened the newspaper to the classifieds.

One afternoon, I spotted a posting for data entry clerks. They were looking for people who could type fast and knew their way around a computer. That sounded like me. I'd always been good at typing, I was a trained classical pianist and had taken typing in school, and I'd been fascinated with computers for as long as I could remember. I took every computer class offered in high school, so I felt confident I'd get the job.

I called the number listed, and they told me to come the next day for an aptitude test. It turned out to be a temp-to-hire agency, and when I arrived, I was greeted by a familiar face, Lori.

I had known her since I was little; she went to my church and once ran a small business with my mom. They told me that I got the job and if I did very well, they would offer me a permanent position in ninety days. The only bad thing was that I wasn't guaranteed a particular shift. It was dependent on their needs, it was check processing, so at the end of the month we would be stuck there until all the checks had been cleared. I was working sixty-five, sometimes seventy hours a week.

As I began the new job, my aunt asked me to lunch and brought it to my attention that my son wasn't acting like typical kids. We had attended her grandson's birthday party, and someone there noticed that my son wasn't interacting with the other kids, nor was he interested in playing with the toys. That was the first time I heard the term 'autism'. She told me to take some time to research it online and if I felt that he had the symptoms, I should contact his doctor.

I went home and immediately started researching what autism was. Suddenly, everything began to make sense.

My son used to love bath time, and now he screamed bloody murder every time I tried to bathe him. For a while, I thought maybe something had happened while he was visiting his other Grandma, maybe the water had been too hot, or he had fallen, and no one told me, but nothing checked out. He also went from eating spaghetti and other foods to absolutely refusing them. His language was delayed, and he was fascinated by inanimate objects like shoestrings, and by opening and closing doors repeatedly.

The more I read, the more my heart sank. It felt like puzzle pieces were locking into place, but it was a picture I wasn't ready to see. I made an appointment with his pediatrician; the same one I had growing up. My mom came with me for support.

As I explained my concerns, the doctor seemed uninterested, even dismissive. She accused me of overreacting, of not being able to handle being a teenage mom. I looked her straight in the

eye and said, "If there's nothing to be concerned about, then why has my son been opening and closing that cabinet door for the past fifteen minutes while we've been talking?"

She glanced at me, then over at my son, and her expression changed. Bewilderment crossed her face as she said, "I'll be right back with some papers."

She had provided papers and a referral for us to go to Easter Seals for testing. Please remember that back in 2002 autism diagnosis was quite different. The estimate was about 1 in 150 children being identified with autism. Fast forward to today and it's around 1 in 31 children, among boys, roughly one in twenty-five to one in twenty.

My son was officially diagnosed with Pervasive Developmental Disorder, or

PDD, which placed him on the autism spectrum. At the time, PDD was a broad diagnostic category used for children who showed differences in social, communication, and behavioral development. Today, that diagnosis falls under Autism Spectrum Disorder (ASD).

The specialists told me there was a chance he might never speak like the average child. They also explained that his struggles with bath time and his dislike of swinging were related to sensory processing issues. A treatment plan was created for him that included speech, occupational, physical, and sensory integration therapy.

Hearing the diagnosis was one thing but living it was another. I was working full time, sometimes long hours, just trying to keep everything together. My mom helped when she could, and from time to time, therapists came to our home, but most of his appointments had to be in person. His therapy center was thirty minutes away, and he needed several different sessions every week.

I didn't always feel capable. I was often tired from working so much, but I showed up anyway, or my mom took him when I couldn't.

As if that wasn't enough to handle, Josh decided to take me to court to secure visitation. I had never told him he couldn't see his son, and now I was faced with the stress of legal proceedings on top of everything else. It felt unfair and exhausting, like one more test I hadn't signed up for. I was determined to protect his stability, no matter what it took.

Josh and I eventually agreed on visitation, but it quickly became clear that it was too much for him to handle. He was still a teenager himself, trying to figure out who he was, and now he had a child with special needs. The reality of that responsibility was something he wasn't ready for and once again removed himself from our lives.

Once my son reached the age of three, I was able to get him enrolled in a special school for children with special needs and developmental delays. This gave him much more one on one time for therapy and the structure he desperately needed.

By age six, he was mainstreamed into public school where he thrived and was on the honor roll several times and learned to play electric guitar.

Reflection
Trusting Yourself

There are moments when something inside you knows the truth before anyone else does. Even when you're tired, overwhelmed, or unsure, that quiet knowing keeps nudging you forward. This season reminded me that being dismissed doesn't mean you're wrong. Sometimes it's the very thing that teaches you to trust yourself, speak up, and keep going when everything feels heavy.

A Note to You

Trust yourself. If something feels off, it's worth paying attention to. You don't need permission, proof, or anyone else's approval to take yourself seriously.

Rebel Rising

What is one thing your gut has been trying to tell you lately, and what would it look like to trust yourself enough to act on it?

Chapter 7

Walking Into My Future

One evening around Christmas, I decided to go to Walmart to find a gift for my parents. DVD players had just come out, and while I didn't know much about them, I knew they were supposed to be better than a VCR.

As I was walking toward the cashier to check out, you'll never guess who I ran into. Damon. Yes, *that* Damon — the one who had bullied me and ruined my reputation just as I was trying to build one. My heart sank. He was cuter than ever, but all I could think about was just keep walking and hope he didn't notice me.

"Janice!" He yelled.
 Nope. Didn't go unnoticed.

"Hey," I replied, keeping my pace. He jogged up beside me and started walking with me.

"How've you been? It's been a really long time."

I couldn't believe he was really going to do the small talk thing with me. But me being polite, I stopped walking and talked with him for a bit. He was charming, cute, and surprisingly sincere. Maybe it was time to forgive him. Maybe his actions back then were just the mistakes of a stupid teenage boy.

He invited me to go to another store nearby, and I agreed. After that, he asked me to come hear his little brother play at a local bar. I forgot to mention his brother was best friends with my brother at the time. So, I agreed to go.

My mom tried to talk me out of it. "He's a jerk, Janice. Remember what happened?" she warned. I really should have listened to her.

I went to the bar. He never showed up.

I remember sitting there, feeling embarrassed and a little angry at myself for believing he might have changed. Maybe that was the closure I needed, a reminder that some people stay exactly who they were.

Not long after that, I met a girl at work named Rachael. One evening, we were all waiting in the break room for the previous shift to finish before we could start ours, and we started chatting.

She asked where I was from, and we were both shocked to realize we'd gone to the same high school. She had graduated just a year before I did. To make it even more ironic, she had dated Josh's best friend while Josh and I were together, but somehow, our paths had never crossed until now.

We hit it off immediately and became inseparable. We sat next to each other every day, worked long hours together, partied together, you name it.

About a year after we met, Rachael and her longtime boyfriend broke up, and she quickly started seeing someone new. She was immediately infatuated with him, and their relationship moved fast.

Before long, she was always with him and his friend Jason and his fiancée. Every day at work, Rachael would come in talking about her new boyfriend and Jason, this, Jason that, Jason everything. I was so over hearing about Jason.

In addition to being sick and tired of hearing Rachael talk about Jason, I was also sick of living at home. My parents and I weren't getting along very well, and I was craving independence. That's when, at the age of twenty, I decided to buy my own home.

I told my dad I was going to buy a house, and he wasn't exactly thrilled about it. I didn't have any help with the process other than my realtor. I couldn't afford much, but that was fine for me. I knew buying would be smarter than renting, and I didn't want to move too far from my parents since they were still helping me with my son.

Eventually, I found a small, foreclosed home that needed a ton of work. When my mom first saw it, she thought I was out of my mind. It reeked cat pee; the flooring was ruined, the plumbing was bad, and the fixtures were outdated. Still, I saw potential.

I had just enough extra money to replace the flooring and update a few fixtures, but I had no idea who to turn for plumbing. When I mentioned it to Rachael, she told me that Jason was a plumber and could probably help me out. She also mentioned that he had just broken up with his fiancée.

Since Rachael was always talking about Jason, I knew he was a hard worker. He had been installing plumbing for new home builds for a few years, and sadly, his dad had recently passed away very suddenly. He had been engaged to his girlfriend, but she had cheated on him.

Rachael described him as kind, family-oriented, and dependable, and only a couple of years older than me. She arranged for Jason to come over and look at my new house.

I'll never forget him pulling up in his little truck. He was a couple of inches shorter than I expected, tanned from working in the summer sun. Worn jeans, work boots, a white tank top. He was better looking than I expected, very fit, with a smile that reached his bluish-hazel eyes.

Jason did a walkthrough of the house, and to my dismay, the entire plumbing system needed to be replaced. The home had been sitting for years and was a complete mess. Knowing I was a single mom, he offered to do all the work for free if I could cover the cost of supplies. I couldn't believe how kind he was.

Later that night, Rachael called and told me Jason thought I was pretty and wanted to know if I'd be interested in going out with him. I told her I'd think about it and give him my number so we could talk first. He called that night, and we hit it off immediately. We talked for hours and decided to double date that weekend at a local bar with Rachael and her husband.

We had a blast that night. We played pool, and I beat him pretty good. He had no idea I'd grown up playing and could hold my own. I was only twenty, but Rachael's husband worked at the bar, so it was easy for me to get in and have a few drinks. It became our go-to hangout, and Jason and I continued seeing each other. We celebrated my twenty-first birthday there, and not long after, I started bartending part-time.

Jason and I were inseparable. I was either at his place, or he was at mine. He loved my son and my son loved him. But I was getting burned out on my data entry job. It was monotonous, with no real opportunity to grow, so I switched to part-time and bartended. It only made sense for Jason to move in; I owned my home, and paying both his rent and my mortgage didn't seem practical.

Once he moved in, though, it quickly became clear that Jason drank a lot. He always had an excuse, usually saying it was because he was grieving his dad's death. When I bartended, he would sit at the bar and drink, often spending the same money I'd just earned in tips. I eventually decided to quit, hoping it would help him cut back. He always told me that once we got married, he would stop.

Now that we lived together, marriage became a regular topic of conversation, and we celebrated one year together. My son was getting older, and I wanted him to have a sibling who wasn't too young. He was five now, and I was starting to imagine what our future as a family could look like.

Jason and I decided it would be a good idea to take his former fiancé's engagement ring and trade it in toward mine. So, we made an appointment at the local jewelry store, traded the ring, and picked out what would become mine. Within a couple of hours, they had it resized and ready to go. I was over the moon.

I'll never forget sitting beside my son's bed that night, waiting for him to fall asleep as I did every night, staring at the beautiful, shiny ring on my finger. It wasn't anything elaborate, but it was the nicest piece of jewelry I had ever owned.

A half-carat princess cut diamond with two small marquise stones on each side, set in white gold. It never even crossed my mind that he hadn't officially proposed. We were getting married.

Reflection
Believing What You Want to See

Sometimes we don't ignore the warning signs because we don't see them. We ignore them because we want the story to turn out differently this time. When someone shows up with kindness, attention, or possibility, it's easy to fill in the blanks ourselves.

A Note to You

Wanting things to work doesn't make you naïve. It makes you human. Just don't abandon your intuition to keep a dream alive.

Rebel Rising

Take your time with this on the next page.

Where have you trusted potential or hope over what you were experiencing? What did your intuition notice before you were ready to listen?

Chapter 8

We're Getting Married!

As soon as the ring was on my finger, all I could think about was planning our wedding. We immediately told our families, and while he was at work, I started researching where we could have our wedding. We lived in a very small town, and there wasn't that much to choose from, and everyone knows the ceremony itself isn't the focal point, it's the reception party.

I found the perfect place to host it. The problem was they only had one date available for the following year, April fifteenth, just nine months away, and Tax Day! It also happened to be Easter weekend that year.

Now we had to find someone to marry us. We didn't belong to any church, and even though we were non-denominational Christians, most churches wouldn't marry us unless we were members. That hurt me deeply. Nowhere in the Bible does God say you must belong to a church to get married. I wasn't going to join a church just to be married there, that didn't feel right. So, we decided to have our ceremony in a hotel ballroom, and my parents' minister agreed to officiate.

Nine months flew by. I'd love to say Jason's drinking got better, but it didn't. The promise of "Once we get married, I'll stop drinking," turned into "Once we have kids, I'll quit."

The day before the wedding, everything that had been coming together perfectly started to fall apart. Sometimes a string of small disasters feels like an omen, and maybe this was one.

The florist ran short on flowers; I had ordered calla lilies, but we didn't have enough for all the bouquets and boutonnieres. When Mom and I went to the reception hall to check on the setup and drop off the liquor for the open bar, everything was completely wrong: the colors, the centerpieces, the tables.

I asked a woman setting up if there was another wedding before ours, and she said, "No, this is for your wedding." My heart sank. We tracked down the owner, who assured us everything would be fixed.

Then came another blow: my brother, who was in the Marines, wasn't going to be able to come home after all. I had been counting on him being there. The stress was overwhelming.

The day of the wedding arrived, and as I stood outside the hotel ballroom, shaking like a leaf, the worst words a bride could hear hit me: "Jason isn't here."

No. This can't be happening. No. No. No.

Rachael, my maid of honor, best friend, and matchmaker, didn't hesitate. "I'll go find him," she said, and ran out. Ten minutes felt like a lifetime. When she returned, she told me Jason had been too busy drinking with his groomsmen to realize it was time for the ceremony.

I'll never forget those ten minutes. They linger with me even now. I knew in my gut that marrying him wasn't the right decision, but I walked forward anyway.

I wish I could say the reception went off without a hitch, but I'd be lying. My in-laws were introduced incorrectly by the DJ, a key song I wanted wasn't played, an uninvited guest hugged me only to spill her mixed cola drink all down my back and my gown, the bar was shut down before I could even get a drink, and to make matters worse, when we arrived to the hotel for our wedding night, one of Jason's groomsmen was belligerently drunk and he and Jason got into a fight.

I realized quickly that our marriage wasn't starting off on the right foot, but I told myself that was normal. Not everything is smooth in the beginning.

Still, the pressure kept piling on. I wanted another baby right away, and I needed my brother in law out of my house right away too. Thankfully, God answered that prayer quickly. He found another family member to stay with while he tried to repair his own marriage.

I talked to Jason about wanting to try for a baby. He wasn't sure at first, but I explained that because I had an IUD, I'd need to make an appointment to have it removed, and it might take a while before we could conceive. He eventually agreed.

I made the appointment, and the doctor cleared me to begin trying. I was nervous because I had lost a baby a couple years prior, but to my surprise, I became pregnant almost immediately. I hatched a plan to tell Jason by surprising him with a teddy bear that would be for our new baby, a bib that said, "I love my Daddy", and I secured my pregnancy test to the teddy bear's arm. When I told him, he couldn't believe it. He was happy, but not quite the happy I had been hoping for.

A couple of weeks later I miscarried, it was June 6th, 2006. A day I will never forget. I felt that loss so deeply. No one around me could understand how I felt.

No one I knew had miscarried, let alone twice. I was inconsolable and Jason wasn't as supportive as I had hoped. I laid in bed next to my husband, writhing in so much pain as he slept. Feeling the loss mentally and physically, deeper than anyone could understand, and once again alone.

I prayed harder that night than I ever had before. I begged God to give me more children. I wanted so desperately for my son to have siblings, to have other children, and to finally feel settled.

God answered my prayers. We became pregnant again quickly. In fact, I spent most of 2006, 2007, 2008, and 2009 pregnant, and I gave birth to three beautiful sons. In 2009, Josh signed his parental rights over so Jason could formally adopt my oldest son.

I wish I could say that things continued to be happy and stable, but unfortunately the vision I had of a happy family wasn't the one we would have.

Initially it looked that way. Jason and I would take the kids down to my parents to watch football on Sundays. But for the most part and as the years went on, Jason drank more and more, up to thirty beers a day, and eventually he made a decision that brought our world to a crashing halt.

Reflection
When "Forever" Starts to Fray

Sometimes we hope something will last forever, whether that's a friendship, relationship or career. Unfortunately, that's not how things work, but often we live in denial, especially when we are so busy holding it all together.

A Note to You

You may still be standing in the middle of your own "forever" ending, but don't lose heart. Every ending you survive becomes the foundation of your strength and the person you are rising to be.

Rebel Rising

Take your time with this on the next page.

Think about the last time something you felt certain would last forever came to an end.

What did it teach you about the difference between what you want and what you truly need?

Chapter 9

The Crashing Halt

Jason and I married in 2006, and by 2008, after the birth of our second son, I began to feel an overwhelming loneliness.

Jason would work, come home, drink, and pass out, or he'd come home and leave again with a friend. I was left to take care of three children entirely on my own, and to make things more difficult, we were down to one car at the time.

On Thanksgiving in 2008, I started having severe stomach pain. My dad took me to the ER and left me there for testing. They admitted me with appendicitis. It was my first surgery.

The hospital was cold, quiet, and empty. I was in pain, scared, and worried, and once again, utterly alone. No one came before the surgery. No one came after. Not until it was time to pick me up.

When I came home to recover, I once again found myself alone, tending to three children. That was when I decided I wanted a divorce. I sat Jason down and told him I couldn't live like this anymore. It wasn't fair to me or to the kids. He began to cry, begging me not to give up on our marriage or break up our family. Then he left the house.

I assumed he was going to his friends to drink, but to my surprise, he went straight to my parents. There, he put all the blame on me. He told them false stories about how I couldn't manage money, when the truth was that most of it was being poured into booze.

We "separated" for about a month, even while living in the same house. I was a stay-at-home mom at the time, and honestly, where was I going to go?

To my surprise, around Christmas time I found out I was pregnant again.

I wish I could say I was excited, but I wasn't. It couldn't have come at a worse time. I found myself questioning everything.

My morals, my faith, my ability to keep doing this. But in the end, I knew what I had to do. I decided to keep working on my marriage and prepare to have the baby.

After my fourth son was born, it became apparent that we needed more money. Three kids in diapers and on special formula is no easy feat.

I began doing some marketing work from home and had taken some college courses. Jason had the opportunity to launch his own business, subcontracting for another plumbing company, that meant more money and something I could help him with. But, once again, as more money came in, the drinking increased.

Fourth of July was when I realized I couldn't do this to my children anymore. Jason had passed out on our living room floor. Our four-year-old son sitting on top of him crying for Daddy to wake up to watch fireworks, broke my heart in two. The next day I told Jason I thought it would be best for him to go and find his own apartment.

He moved out for a couple of months, and then, like before, we tried to work things out. He moved back in, still paying rent on his apartment. One day he came home from work with blood gushing from his nose. I grabbed a large food storage bowl from the cabinet, and within moments it was half full. We needed to get to the ER fast.

At the hospital, Jason's mom met us there. We were both terrified. The nurse kept asking if Jason had snorted or used any drugs. He fiercely denied it. The more she asked, the more suspicious I became. Finally, she looked right at me and said, "The only time I've ever seen this happen is when someone has snorted a hard drug and ruptured their blood vessels." They sent him home with a balloon in his nose and an appointment to see a specialist.

Things only got worse after that. Jason reeked of alcohol constantly. Our bedroom smelled like it. No matter how much I cleaned, the odor never went away. I began sleeping on the couch because when he was drunk and angry, he would lash out.

My breaking point came around Christmas. I remember sobbing, crying out to God. I wanted to get a divorce but was consumed with guilt. I had promised to make the marriage work, but it couldn't work if I was the only one trying.

At that moment, a televangelist came on the TV, talking about how Christians often judge those who are divorcing. He said, "You never know the battles those people are facing or how difficult that decision was for them." That hit me hard.

I realized that staying in this toxic marriage, especially in its current state, would be far more damaging for my children to grow up witnessing. It's funny how God finds ways to speak to us in our moments of deep despair.

Once again, Jason moved out, and I began filing paperwork to end our marriage.

The final confirmation that I was making the right decision came with a knock on my door. When I opened it, our business partner was standing there. He asked if Jason was home. I told him no, that I'd kicked Jason out over his drinking. That's when he told me the truth. Jason had been stealing supplies from the company and selling them to other suppliers to get money for OxyContin.

He had been snorting Oxy.

The shockwave that went through me was felt physically. Everything started to make perfect sense. The missing money, the change in his personality, the late nights. The person I had once known and loved had disappeared. A true Jekyll and Hyde.

Jason and I agreed to a dissolution. He moved into a larger apartment so he could have the kids for visitation, and I split a great deal of our furniture, the boys' toys, and their gaming systems.

For a while, everything seemed to be going fine, until one day, I picked the kids up after a visit.

Our four-year-old son looked up at me with his big, beautiful blue eyes, his golden curls tousled around his face, and said, "Daddy punched me in the face."

I couldn't believe my ears. There was a red mark on his cheek. Being alone and not wanting to escalate the situation, I immediately took the kids and left.

That night, I decided that if Jason wanted to see the boys, it would have to be at our home, and I told him that.

He agreed and didn't seem to have a real issue with it.

He never came. He's never seen them since.

Reflection

Choosing Yourself Isn't Always Easy

Sometimes we already know the truth long before we act on it. We hold on, hoping things will change, convincing ourselves that love or effort or faith will be enough to fix what's broken. But the rebel within us knows better. She's the one who finally says, "I can't keep losing myself trying to make this work."

A Note to You

The moment you stop waiting for someone else to change and start protecting your own peace is the moment your rebellion begins. Choosing yourself isn't selfish; it's sacred.

Rebel Rising

When was a time you knew the truth deep down but kept hoping it would turn out differently? What finally pushed you to take the leap and choose yourself anyway?

____

____

____

____

____

____

____

____

____

____

____

____

____

____

____

____

____

Chapter 10

The Next Act

Coming out of that marriage, I was ready to focus on myself, find my love, and have a career. I was twenty-eight years old and, for the first time in a long time, I felt free. Even though so much was still uncertain, that freedom felt intoxicating.

I threw myself into working out. I lost thirty pounds and became determined to keep it off, maybe a little too determined. Somewhere along the way, it shifted from healthy motivation to obsession.

I started weighing myself several times a day, tracking every fluctuation. It reminded me of my teenage years, after my first son was born, when I became fixated on hitting one hundred pounds at that time. I'm five foot eight inches, so that goal was dangerously thin.

Back then, and now again, it wasn't really about the number. It was about control, the one thing I could cling to when everything else in my life felt unpredictable.

I began dating again and met a man eight years my senior, his name was Dave. He had been divorced for a couple of years, had a daughter, and a good job as a branch manager of a national lawn care company.

In Dave, I found someone with stability, maturity, experience, a good, responsible parent, and who made me laugh, feel good about myself, seen and confident.

He lived nearby in a small apartment, and coming out of the marriage I had been in prior; it was important to me that he wasn't a heavy drinker.

One day Dave invited me over to his house and asked if I wanted something to drink. He opened the bottom of his refrigerator drawer, and it was full of beer. I asked him why he had so much and if he drank on a regular basis.

He assured me that he did not and that he only had all that beer in there because he had moved into his apartment not long ago, and the guys from work came over with a bunch of beer.

Dave and I would have fun, we would go to eat, listen to my friends' band play at the local bar, go watch a movie and most of all, Dave liked to shop for me. I didn't know what that was like.

Before, my world revolved around survival, making sure my kids were fed and had what they needed. So, having someone take me out, buy me things, and make me feel special was new.

A couple of months in, Dave had a big idea that we should go on a vacation together. I hadn't been on vacation for years and he wanted to go to Miami. I had never been.

I was feeling a little apprehensive. I had never left the kids for that long, and even though I knew they would be safe with my parents, I was scared. I also hadn't flown since I was six years old, so flying and being afraid of heights terrified me.

He had booked the flight and the hotel and shared it with me. I looked online at the reviews of the hotel and they were awful! They were talking about locks being broken, rooms being broken into, and items being stolen from their hotel. It didn't look or sound safe at all.

That's when I decided I would not be going, and Dave did not take that news very well. We ended up in a horrible fight; terrible things were said and left so mad at me.

After speaking the next day, he understood why I was cautious and afraid, and agreed to go somewhere we could drive to, and we settled on Myrtle Beach, SC.

It was my first time visiting Myrtle Beach, South Carolina. Rachael went every year, but I never had. Since my grandma lived in Maryland, our family vacations had always been to Ocean City.

South Carolina felt different, the air, the energy, even the people. I loved it.

Dave and I spent our days wandering through little shops and trying new restaurants near the hotel. After four months of dating, we finally said our *I love you's*. One night, after a fun dinner and sharing a big island-themed drink, Dave started talking about our future, how one day we'd get married and have a beautiful daughter together.

I just sat there, stunned. He already had a daughter, and I hadn't planned on having any more children. Marriage again? That wasn't something I was sure I ever wanted to do. But he spoke with such confidence, as if it had already been decided. It left me spinning, part of me flattered, part of me uneasy, and all of me with a lot to think about.

The next day we were out exploring and happened across an aquarium. We stood in front of their desk that had an elaborate awning and prices. He was looking down at the different packages and looked at me and asked what I wanted to do, and I said I didn't mind; it was up to him. For some reason, this made him angry, and we went back and forth. For anyone who knows me, I'm easygoing. I was just trying to let him take the lead. But instead, it became an argument.

When we went back to the hotel, it was cold and quiet between us. He decided to get on the phone to speak with his daughter, and I decided to head out across the street to a beachwear store so I could call my mom. When I returned, he was upset that I had left and worried about my safety. I assured him that I was fine and had stayed close by. We made up and headed up the following day.

Shortly after we had returned from that trip, Dave and I began talking about him moving in. Money was very tight for me, a newly single mom. In my dissolution agreement, the mortgage remained in Jason's name on our home, but I would stay and pay for it, so the kids had a place to live. Jason was nowhere to be found, so it was up to me to provide, and I started working a temporary job at a retail store, but it was tough, and Dave knowing that pointed out it would be far more affordable for me if he moved in. This was just six months into our relationship.

The following month, my maternal grandmother suddenly passed away. I was gut wrenched. After spending many years at a nursing home due to her complicated health, she had just moved closer to home a few months prior, and now she was suddenly gone.

After attending her funeral alone, I came home and was still grieving, while Dave had made himself a drink and was acting like everything was normal. When I said something about how I felt he told me to stop being a drama queen. His words cut deep. I was craving compassion and comfort but found neither in him.

Not too long after my grandmother's passing, we were having dinner and watching a movie, when he received a mysterious text. He said someone had a gun that he had lent them, and he needed to go pick it up. He was gone for a few hours, and when he returned, his knuckles were bloodied. He said a fight had ensued over the gun, and the guy didn't want to give it back, and seemed very suspicious. To this day, I'm not entirely certain of the true story of that night.

Things began to improve though, the fights were fewer, and we began talking about getting married. For me, being a Christian and living with someone without getting married just wasn't something I felt right about.

He convinced me that in order to buy me an engagement ring we should sell mine from my first marriage, and so I did. I sometimes regret that, perhaps it would have been something I could have given to one of my sons, but I was twenty-eight years old, and I felt I was being pushed into selling it, and a part of me wanted to start fresh.

This time, I received an official proposal. We went down to visit my grandmother in Ocean City, Maryland, and Dave asked me to take him to one of my favorite spots on the beach. The evening was warm, with a subtle breeze, and the sun was just beginning to set. As I stood there looking out at the ocean, he got down on one knee and asked me to marry him.

I said yes, just as one of his flip-flops slipped off and floated away into the surf. An omen, perhaps.

After that, we started talking about what kind of wedding we wanted. I had already done the big, traditional wedding, and since this was a second marriage for both of us, we wanted something simpler. For a while, we tossed around the idea of going to Las Vegas. I even went out and bought a beautiful trumpet-style gown for the occasion.

But right around my twenty-ninth birthday, Dave started having second thoughts. It didn't make sense to me. Eventually, he changed his mind again, and instead of Vegas, we decided on a beach wedding in May, just six months away.

May arrived, and I sat in the car next to Dave in my blush-colored satin dress holding my bouquet. I was quietly reflecting on my decision, and remembering how, just seven years earlier, I had made my first decision to get married. I asked myself if I was certain this time, and how I felt. I felt calm. I felt sure. The man sitting next to me, though, I wasn't so sure about. He seemed distant, almost pensive.

When it was time to meet the officiant on the beach, the area had been cleared just for us. It was only Dave and me, with a few people watching from the pier above. We chose to do a sand ceremony, mine coral, his blue, and poured them together to symbolize our unity. Afterward, the officiant took our photos, and for a little while, we laughed and had fun.

But the moment was short-lived. That night, I wanted to go to a romantic restaurant to celebrate. When we arrived, the line was long, and Dave didn't want to wait. He made us walk several blocks to another place, but that one had to wait too. Frustrated, he refused to stay, and we ended up back at the hotel eating frozen pizza and wings. Before the night was over, we were in another argument, over something small, but it felt much bigger.

Reflection
Trusting Our Gut

Sometimes our gut knows before we can explain why. When things look good on the surface, it's easy to ignore that quiet hesitation and tell yourself you're being dramatic. But that small feeling, the pause, the unease, is information. Learning to trust yourself starts with letting what feels off matter.

A Note to You

If you felt it, there was a reason. You don't need proof to take yourself seriously.

Rebel Rising

Take your time with this on the next page.

When was the last time you trusted your gut, and what helped you lean into it?

Chapter 11

Honeymoon's Over

When we returned home, there wasn't a honeymoon phase. We didn't receive cards or congratulations from anyone but my parents. I was still working at my retail job and wasn't very happy. I knew it was a temporary position while I sought out something more, and preferably back in marketing. That's when opportunity struck.

Remember the recruiting company that hired me after high school? Well, they were hiring someone to help recruit and market their location. Lori still worked there and was more than happy to bring me on.

It felt good to be back in an office setting and in the marketing world. I learned very quickly and launched social media pages that the company didn't have. I built a social media strategy and started marketing our open jobs. It did extremely well and was especially successful in finding people to fill our blue-collar roles.

I had just turned thirty, and while I had started college years before, I hadn't finished. So, I decided to go back. For a while, everything was going well. But over time, I started to notice behavior in Lori that made me uneasy. She showed clear bias in hiring, turning away qualified candidates because of personal feelings. It bothered me deeply.

One day I accidentally texted my co-worker about Lori and how uneasy I felt about it. Only to realize I accidentally sent it to Lori. I was utterly humiliated. She made me stay after work, locked me in the office, and threatened to fire me. There were times I would be typing a message; she would slap my hand off my keyboard and yell at me, telling me I was doing it all wrong. She was the definition of a micro-manager and a toxic boss. Worse yet, she had been a family friend, which made it harder to process and even harder to leave.

The months went on, and I endured the micromanagement while also attending college and doing my coursework in the evenings. Then one day, I became very ill. Doctors found a node on my vocal cords that caused me to lose my voice. They couldn't say how long recovery would take. After talking it over with my husband, we decided it would be best for me to resign for the time being.

 A couple of months later, Lori called, asking how my health was. I told her I was doing better, I started to regain my voice, the node was going down considerably, and she asked if I would return to work for her, I told her no.

As scary as the health crisis was, I felt like God was pulling me away from her to protect me. Even in the chaos, He had kept me safe, and this was my chance to walk in that truth instead of going back to what broke me.

Things with Dave, unfortunately, stayed the same during this time, periods of calm followed by chaos, and then back again. Being off work made me anxious; I didn't like the feeling of having no control. And as if that wasn't enough, a couple of months later, I was shocked to find out I was pregnant. Honestly, I'm not sure why I was so shocked. I wasn't on birth control, and didn't do anything to prevent it, however, it was still shocking, and I was much older than the last time I had gone through it. Dave was surprised but handled it well. We both hoped for a girl, I already had four boys after all, and he had a daughter.

We were blessed with a baby girl on New Year's Day, 2015. She came into the world in a rush, so quickly that there wasn't even time for pain medication. Dave stood by, completely stunned. No encouragement, no words of comfort, just shock.

When we brought our daughter home, I didn't want to be without her. For weeks, I stayed locked in our room with her.

Having her changed everything for me. I had a daughter. I still couldn't believe it. As a boy mom, I can say, having a girl is very different. You feel protective in a deeper way than you do with a boy.

Dave would leave for work in the mornings while I got the boys off to school, cared for my baby girl and successfully breastfed her, while I kept up with my college coursework. But around seven months after her birth, I started to feel a deep pull, a calling, to return to work. So, just for fun, I started looking. I came across a position that immediately caught my eye: Account Executive for our local TV station. Looking back, that pull I felt was God. Taking this job changed my entire career path.

I landed the job very quickly and it was extremely surreal. I grew up wanting to work at the local TV station, ever since I had met the news woman at our school. Now, here I was, working with the local TV station, attending their Christmas party at the local country club and seeing all the local famous faces I had seen on TV. I couldn't believe this was real life.

The hours worked well; it was close to home, and Mom would watch our daughter while Dave and I worked. That is, until one day, I came home to find that Dave had abruptly quit his job.

He said he wanted to be a stay-at-home dad now. I was in disbelief. He had never discussed this with me. While my salary covered the bills, his income gave us stability, and without it, everything fell on me.

How would he pay his child support, his credit cards, or his car? Suddenly, that all became my responsibility.

For a couple of years Dave and I talked about moving to Myrtle Beach. When I was pregnant, we had even made the journey down there, looked at apartments and houses, and explored transferring his job there, but ultimately decided it wasn't the right time with the kids still being so young and now expecting, having my family nearby was a comfort.

Working at the TV station was great, for the most part. But it was very much a *good ol' boys club.* Most of the media world is. One of my agency clients, a former general manager of our station, was especially abusive.

Once, he wanted a TV commercial swapped out because the woman in it had passed away. I'd done everything on my end to have it changed, but the station hadn't processed it fast enough. That Saturday, at 11 o'clock at night, he called and cursed me over it. Sadly, this kind of behavior was common, and tolerated by my bosses.

So, I started looking elsewhere. One of our sister stations happened to be in Myrtle Beach, South Carolina. I applied for their Senior Account Executive position and had to let my bosses know, which they didn't take well. A few days later, I got a call from the sales manager in Myrtle Beach; they wanted to fly me down for an interview.

I couldn't believe it. Remember how terrified I was flying? Well, I was going to do this, and I was going to do it by myself.

Reflection

Being Brave

Being brave isn't always obvious. We often do it without even realizing or giving ourselves the proper credit we should. Many times, we are forced into it, instead of cowardice. These moments deserve attention for you to see how incredible you are.

A Note to You

You may feel like you haven't been very brave. Maybe you thought you could be more so. Just know, it's enough either way.

Rebel Rising

Take your time with this on the next page.

What is one difficult moment you had a choice to walk away from or bravely face head on?

Chapter 12

The Destination

I bravely boarded the plane just after six in the morning, still dark outside. The airport was eerily quiet like it gets before sunrise. My nerves were an absolute wreck. I barely remembered what it was like to be on a plane. I was praying so hard, the irrational thoughts were swirling, and so was my stomach. I didn't drink coffee or eat anything before I left because of it.

When I arrived in Myrtle Beach, I had just enough time to get my rental car and get to my interview. My manager I was meeting assured me that they would have a hotel for me, so there would be nothing to worry about. The TV station was much smaller than I had anticipated, smaller in size than the one I was currently at but it was a bigger market. That's how the world of TV works. Each station is ranked on the size of their market. I was currently working in one of the smallest markets, and this was a sizable change.

When I walked into the building, it was a cold waiting room and there was a woman at the window that reminded me of the lady behind the counter with bleached hair and purple tips who greeted me and said she would grab David, the manager.

The woman was nice, David introduced her as Tami and said she was new to the station. Tami began to talk to me about her job, the station, and was carrying on like I didn't have any experience when I had been at my current job for a year. David interjected and told her just that. She wished me luck and headed out on her merry way.

David tried talking to me some more, asking why I wanted the job, why I wanted to move to South Carolina, did I have any family there, what did my family think of the move, how did work feel about it, all the questions, then another knock at the door.

A short woman came in, much older than me, short auburn hair, heavy perfume, chopping gum obnoxiously, another strong southern accent, and this one had quite the attitude. Her name was April. She was managing most of the auto accounts, and she was really upset about spots not airing when they were supposed to.

Once she left, David realized that being there was too difficult for us to discuss privately, so we went to lunch. It was a nice place, in a quaint little town located outside of Myrtle Beach. I just ordered some bread since I wasn't feeling well, the more he talked, the worse I felt. I excused myself to the bathroom and ended up vomiting profusely. Once I returned to the table, David could see I did not look well and offered to take me back to the station to grab my rental car and find a hotel, because he had forgotten to book it.

Once I finally arrived in my hotel room, I collapsed onto the bed. I missed my kids terribly. Did I make a huge mistake coming here?

I called my family and filled them in on my day, ordered some food, went to bed, and couldn't wait to get on the plane the next day to come home.

David had me scheduled to come into the station one more time before my departure. This time, our meeting was rather short, the role they had available was essentially the same I was currently doing, but it didn't come with a big book of business, which meant not as much money as I hoped.

We said goodbye, and I was all too happy to leave. Ready to come home, the nerves I had come down with had left me, excitement in its place.

When I returned to my job back home, I was met with disdain from my bosses. They knew I had been down to Myrtle Beach, and my General Sales Manager had been speaking to them. I wasn't sure what was going to happen. I wasn't entirely sure I wanted that job after meeting with David and some of the women at the station. Now, I felt I was being ostracized because I was looking to move and grow my career, something I knew I couldn't do at that station.

A month later, I noticed that my husband had been acting a little differently, particularly around me getting the mail. One day I got to the mailbox before he could and was shocked and devastated to find a letter from the bank that our home was being foreclosed on.

This had been my home for ten years. The home I had dreamed of as a kid. The home where I come home from birthing four of my five children.

The home was surrounded by relatives and neighbors I loved. I thought Dave had been paying the mortgage. That was the agreement; I worked; he managed the house, bills, kids, everything. That was the deal when he decided to stay home.

But he hadn't been paying for it. And the mortgage wasn't even in my name. It was still in my ex-husband's.

There was no saving it. We had to move and fast.

Somehow, with five kids, I found a house big enough, close to work, affordable, and available immediately. We packed up our lives and left.

Saying goodbye hurt in such a deep way I can still feel it. It wasn't just a house; it was a dream I'd built. I remembered being pregnant with my second son, while my oldest played in his new bedroom. Me removing all the awful old wallpaper border. Painting. Refinishing the floors. The large backyard with the perfect tree for my kids to play.

I focused on the positives. Bigger house. Two and a half baths. Large fenced in yard with a patio. I made the best of it.

My friend Bryan called, remember the one who had stolen the pregnancy test for me. We had kept in touch over the years and hadn't spoken for a while. He had just moved back from Florida, and we agreed to catch up soon.

During that month, I had never heard anything from the station in Myrtle Beach. I had sent an email or two to David but never heard anything back. So, naturally, I assumed they had moved on to another candidate, especially since it wasn't the salary I wanted.

"Janice, it's David from the Myrtle Beach station. If you're still interested in moving down here, we just had another position open. It's over six figures. If you're interested, call me back."

Just like that. Direct. Southern twang and all.

I couldn't believe it. We had just moved. Why now? Why this timing? But the salary was double what I was making. A bigger station. At the beach. How was I supposed to say no?

My husband was immediately against it. Every argument, every excuse, every reason not to go. And I'll admit, those fights got ugly. I wasn't always fair either. I just couldn't believe his reaction. For years he wanted us to move there. Now that it was possibility, he was fighting against it.

But after a lot of back and forth, we agreed. This opportunity could change everything.

One night as we were lying in bed, he grabbed a little white board we had and wrote on it "SC all the way babe!" He was finally on board!

I called David back and said yes. He told me he needed me there in two weeks. I explained we'd just moved, so he reluctantly pushed it to three.

Three weeks to find a new home. Three weeks to sell what we couldn't take.

Three weeks to uproot our entire life, again.

And just like that, we began packing for the next chapter.

Reflection

Making Peace When Life Detours

Sometimes life doesn't go the way we planned, and we find ourselves on detours we never chose. In those moments, it's easy to feel lost or off track. But the truth is, every detour teaches you something about your own resilience and your ability to find a new direction.

A Note to You

You've navigated more unexpected turns than you probably give yourself credit for. Those detours didn't break you; they revealed how adaptable and strong you really are.

Rebel Rising

Think of one detour in your life that ended up teaching you something valuable about yourself. Let yourself notice how that experience shaped your inner rebel.

Chapter 13

Hurricane Season

We found a beautiful temporary beach house on Ocean Blvd. in Surfside Beach, South Carolina. It was a beautiful coral-colored house with ample space, an amazing porch with a view, and perfectly priced for our situation. It was a seasonal rental and fully furnished, which made the idea of uprooting our entire life feel just a little more manageable.

We were moving just two weeks before my birthday. I told myself that starting over in a new place, with a new job and a fresh home, might make this birthday feel different in a good way. I hoped that by the time my birthday came, we would feel settled. I wanted so badly to believe it would be a turning point for our family.

One of the hardest decisions I had to make was about my oldest son. He was already in his sophomore year and moving him that far during such an important stage of school felt too risky. With autism, a dramatic change like that could cause setbacks I did not want him to face.

I sat down with him and explained the situation. He agreed that staying with my parents would be better for him than moving ten hours south and starting over in a new school. I knew he was right, but it still broke something inside me. I wanted to be with all my children, yet I also needed to take the job that would provide a better life for all of us.

I learned that I could not enroll the kids until we were officially moved, so that was something I would have to handle immediately once we settled in. Dave was content being a stay-at-home Dad, so he would continue caring for our daughter.

The next few weeks flew by. We had sold about seventy-five percent of everything we owned. The kids' bikes, all our furniture, and donated anything else we wouldn't have in the beach house.

We promised each other that once we found a permanent home, we would start fresh and furnish it with all new things.

The day we left it was bittersweet. Saying goodbye to our family, friends, and the only place we had known as home.

I felt hopeful, but there was a knot of nerves in my stomach. We took our two vehicles, fully packed with kids, Dave took two of the boys, and I took my second oldest son and our daughter, plus whatever we could fit into my minivan. We left the other half of our stuff at Dave's sister's house. He planned on returning to get it on his own.

A couple of hours into the trip, we saw a double rainbow stretching across the sky. My son pointed to it with wide eyes and said it had to be a sign that everything was going to turn out great. I wanted so badly for him to be right.

Not long after, our daughter, not even two yet, began vomiting repeatedly. She was suffering from terrible motion sickness. We had already planned to stop halfway and stay the night, but now we were stopping constantly to get her and her car seat cleaned up. She would cry and push her brother away when he tried to comfort her, which only made him cry too. It felt like chaos trapped inside a moving car.

By the time we made it to the motel Dave had booked, I was exhausted. The place was far from nice, but I was relieved our daughter could finally rest and get a break from the winding West Virginia mountains that had tormented her little body all day.

The next morning, we left bright and early. We only had about five hours left before reaching our destination, and I was praying that the remainder of the trip would be easier for our daughter, and all of us. Sadly, the sickness continued. By the time we arrived, I was completely drained.

Motherhood doesn't stop, all because you are tired. I still had to get everyone settled into the house. The moment we walked in, I couldn't believe we would be living there. It was one of the most beautiful homes I have ever seen.

The view was gorgeous! We were only one block from the ocean, and our balcony off our master bedroom gave us a great beach view. At night, I could fall asleep to the sound of the waves. For a moment, it felt like a little piece of heaven.

The next day we took a walk on the beach with all the kids. It was amazing to see how our daughter reacted to seeing the ocean for the first time. She was just like her mom, running up and down the shore with her brothers, laughing and giggling. It felt so right at that moment.

On the way back to our house, the boys saw a fishing pier and asked if we could go for a walk on it. I did not have the cash required since I only planned a walk, so I told them the next time we took a walk we would. It was a promise I wouldn't be able to keep.

As we continued walking, I did not notice how uneven the sidewalk was and stubbed my big toe so hard I was certain I had broken it.

Later that evening I called my parents to check on my oldest son, and to let them know we were good. My Dad told me he had just watched the news and saw an alert for a hurricane that was located off the coast. The name was Matthew. Within hours, I started receiving alerts that they were evacuating people in zones A and B inland.

I had no clue what that meant.

What zone were we in?

Does that mean we have to evacuate?

We had just gotten there.

Where are we going to go?

We immediately started searching for a safe place, but everything within a two-hour radius was booked. What had felt surreal and peaceful just hours earlier was turning into a nightmare. Matthew was expected to make landfall the next day.

We eventually found a cheap motel inland; it wasn't as far inland as I would like, but it would keep us from the storm surge that was beginning to make its way in.

We arrived at the motel just in time. The rain and wind was picking up quickly. The six of us crammed in a little tiny, hot, uncomfortable motel room. My toe throbbed with every movement, and to top it all off, a full migraine ensued. The power went out not long after, and we had very little food with us. There was nothing to do except ride it out.

Our only distraction was the gas station across the street. The wind kept lifting the metal awning higher and higher, and we watched it, waiting for the moment it would finally rip away and disappear into the storm. Thankfully, that never happened.

We barely slept that night or the next. When the storm finally calmed down enough that the sun started to peak through the skies again, we decided to attempt to make our way back to our temporary home. I was starting work in two days and staying at the motel was not an option.

The drive was quiet and heavy. The streets were nearly empty, but the debris scattered across the roadway told the real story. Branches, pieces of siding, fallen signs, and broken fragments from people's lives lined our path home. It was a reminder of how loud the days before had truly been.

When we returned home, we were relieved to find no damage to our beach house or belongings. The pier I had promised the kids we would walk on was gone. Completely obliterated. Pieces of it were scattered along the beach for miles. What had been smooth, untouched sand only days earlier was now covered in splintered wood, sharp debris, and broken pieces.

The homes that sat directly on the beach had pools filled with debris, fences torn out of the ground, and yards that looked like they had been churned up by the ocean itself.

After taking in the destruction along the beach, reality set in quickly. I had a new job starting in two days, and ready or not, life was moving forward.

The morning of my new job, I was supposed to meet my manager, David. He arrived late and looked just as disheveled as the first time I met him. He walked me to his office and dropped a bomb I was not ready for. The position I had moved here to take was not exactly available yet.

Remember, April? The short, obnoxious southern woman I had met during my previous interview who managed the auto accounts. She was the one I was hired to replace. The problem was that she was still working there. Not only was she still managing the auto accounts, but she was also going to work for one of our auto clients while still managing her long lists of auto accounts. She was double dipping.

David tried to make it sound like this was a good thing, saying it would give her time to introduce me to the accounts I would eventually take over. But what it really did was create a mess. People were furious when they realized the woman managing their television and digital placements was also working for their competitor, and that the station had never disclosed it.

How did they find out, you may ask?

April showed up at a dealer meeting; this is where the local dealers all gather, and naturally her clients were wondering why she was there. Once they learned the truth, many of them began pulling back their spending or canceling completely, which had a major impact on my commission.

Worse yet, April hated me. She hated that I was a blonde yankee, and in her mind no one was as good as her.

My birthday was coming up, and Dave and I had found a wonderful babysitter, so we decided to go to a local pub just a few blocks from our house. It had a couple of pool tables, good food, and island-themed drinks. I was excited because I loved shooting pool and had not played in a while. We ordered drinks and food, and while we were waiting, I went to use the restroom.

I had locked the door, and while I was in the middle of relieving myself, the bathroom door flew open. To my shock, it was Dave. He was clearly more intoxicated than I was, and I still have no idea what his intention was. The lock must have been broken.

Dave thought it was hilarious and kept opening and closing the door. He finally walked away so I could wash my hands, but when I stepped out of the bathroom, a line of women had gathered and had witnessed the entire thing. None of them looked amused.

I sat down next to him at the bar just as our food arrived. I was upset, but I avoided confrontation. I did not want to address it there or while he was in that condition, so I stayed quiet. Then he leaned close to my ear and whispered, "You are such an asshole." It felt like a knife in my heart.

I was already humiliated, and now he was insulting me for no reason. I asked him why he would say that or what I had done, but he made no sense. He said that if I continued, he would leave me there. I took a drink, and by the time I set my glass down, he was gone.

The place was packed. I looked everywhere for him, but he had disappeared. I paid the bill and walked home alone in the dark, feeling angry, sad, hurt, and utterly bewildered.

The next morning Dave didn't have much to say about the night before. He offered an apology, but I didn't want to hear it. It has crossed a major boundary for me. I told him I needed some time for myself and was going to the beach for some reflection.

I found a quiet place to sit and called my mom. I was devastated and alone. I needed the one person who would listen to what had happened that I knew I could get comfort from.

I had barely been on the phone for fifteen minutes when I saw movement in my peripheral vision. It was Dave, and he had brought all the kids with him. He said they came to get me because he was worried.

The manipulation was obvious. It did not land like he hoped it would. I didn't want the kids to know how upset I was, so I told them I was fine and we walked home. Once we were back, Dave and I went into our bedroom and finally had the conversation I had been holding inside. I looked at him and said words that had been heavy on my heart.

"I don't think this is going to work out. I think it may be better if we divorce."

Reflection

The Shift

There are seasons when everything feels unsettled at once. You're trying to move forward, keep people safe, hold things together, and make the right decisions, all while your body is exhausted, and your heart is on edge. In moments like that, it's easy to minimize what's happening and tell yourself to just push through. Sometimes chaos is the moment you finally realize what you can no longer carry.

A Note to You

If things had to fall apart before you could see clearly, that doesn't mean you waited too long or that you were wrong. It means you were doing the best you could with what you had in the moment.

Rebel Rising

As you think about a season when everything felt too much, notice what it revealed about what you need to feel safe, supported, and respected.

Chapter 14

The Turning Point

After that morning everything shifted. My heart, soul and nervous system, were screaming that being in this marriage, this job, this place, was all a huge mistake. Despite wanting to divorce Dave, I had to be realistic; it wouldn't be the best move right now. Not after we just arrived here. He promised that he would make changes, and I tried my best to immerse myself in work and make new friends.

April was finally leaving the station. Unfortunately, her disdain for me meant that she was going to take her automotive account, the one she now officially worked for, away from me. She made a call to David and threatened to pull their entire spend if they didn't take the account from me and give it to her friend at the station. That one account cost me a great deal of income.

I quickly learned that Tami, the new girl at the station. Was having an affair with our general manager, Ben. Ben didn't like me either, despite my efforts to bring in new business. He wasn't a fan of my being a yankee, especially one that had no ties to Myrtle Beach.

Even with the tension and hostility in the building, I was thriving at work. I had started closing a large six figure digital contract with a local university. I was building strong relationships and proving my value, but none of that mattered to the people who were determined not to like me from the beginning. Success only highlighted how toxic the environment really was. The favoritism Tami and others were receiving was extremely obvious.

The one friend I was able to make at the station was just finalizing her divorce. I was more than happy to have a friend that could understand some of what I was beginning to go through at home. We quickly became thick as thieves. It was just what I needed to make my life at work feel manageable, and I became a safe place for her to turn to with the things she was navigating in her personal life.

Our seasonal rental was coming to an end, and we needed to find a new place to live. After looking at several places, we found a townhome in a private gated community. It was the right size and in the right price range, but it meant another new school for the kids.

A couple of months after moving in, I became extremely sick. It started as what I thought was just a cold and quickly turned into a horrible cough, then sharp stabbing pain. I knew I needed to go to the emergency room. Dave dropped me off so our daughter would not have to sit inside a room full of people. At first, the doctors thought I was having issues with my gallbladder, so they gave me a small dose of pain medication. I am allergic to nearly every pain medication, and it made everything worse. They eventually found pneumonia, not a gallbladder issue.

When it was time to go home, Dave had
to come inside to get me because I had
been given medication. He was livid. I
remember him yelling at me on the
phone about it. I was sick, medicated,
and struggling to stay coherent. He
finally came to pick me up, and once we
returned home, he left me alone with
our daughter to run an errand, even
though I was in no condition to take care
of her.

The pneumonia had taken quite a bit out
of me. I lost over twenty pounds in just
two weeks, and this was just another
reminder of how much our marriage was
failing. Not only did I not have someone
to care for me that I should have but
when I returned to work, when I came
home, I was met with arguing and
nitpicking over the simplest things.

Anytime I suggested that Dave look for a
part time job or do something that
would help him make friends and get
out of the house, he only grew angrier.
The drinking increased as did his
spending of my money while I was at

work, and I was starting to hear from the kids about how aggressive he was toward all of them.

The final straw came in the form of a phone call. Dave had accessed the audio recordings from my phone through my Google account on our computer. He called to confront me, accusing me of cheating. The recording he referenced was a conversation with my manager. I had begun recording meetings because of the issues I was having with management.

That was the moment I knew I could not live like this anymore. I made an appointment with a divorce attorney to understand my options, but the news was bleak. South Carolina's divorce laws were very different from what I expected. We would have to live separately for an entire year before anything could be finalized, and I could not force him to leave the house. Both our names were on the lease, and it did not matter who paid for everything.

He did not work, and he did not want to work. I had been paying his child support for his daughter every month, and that was the only motivation he had to find a job. We shared all our bank accounts, but under my attorney's direction, I withdrew the money and closed the account, giving him no access to my income any longer. That finally pushed him to get a job, but I was still stuck living with him for eight more months until the lease expired.

The environment in our home became volatile. He broke the glass container from our wedding ceremony that held the sand we had poured together. He went through my private belongings and threw away every card he had ever given me. He went through my phone while I was asleep. He flipped me off and cursed me in front of the kids. The tension was constant, and the hostility was unbearable.

Eventually, my friend from work invited me to stay with her for a few weeks until things calmed down. I accepted. I had to.

But her home was not big enough for all of us. It was her and her two kids, plus me and my four. That was too many children in one space. I had no choice but to return home. Dave and I were sleeping separately. He stayed in the Carolina room, and I slept in the master bedroom.

At one point, things got bad again, and a relative who owned a vacation condo in town let us stay there until things settled down at home.

He had finally found a job, but it did not pay enough for him to move out, and it felt intentional. He knew the situation kept me stuck. Things eventually came to a head, and one day he left. He packed his things and drove back home to stay in an empty apartment his ex–mother-in-law had available.

My attorney and I met, and she said because Dave had moved to Ohio, I would still have to file for divorce in South Carolina, at least until Dave met the residency requirements in Ohio, but this made things very complicated.

I remember one night, just crying with all my might on the bathroom floor, praying and asking God why this was happening. Why put me here, just for me to have to leave. It felt like such a failure. I wanted all my life to leave my hometown. I was living where I had dreamed. I had a great job. Why? I did not want to go back home, but I knew I didn't have a choice.

It hadn't even been a year.

Everything I had hoped for shattered.

I called Dave and said, "I'm moving back to Ohio. Let's make this work."

Reflection

The Knowing

There are moments when your body and spirit recognize the truth before your circumstances allow you to act on it. You feel it in your nervous system, in your exhaustion, in the way everything suddenly feels heavier. Knowing doesn't always mean you can leave, fix, or change things right away. Sometimes it simply means you stop lying to yourself about what's happening, and that alone is a powerful turning point.

A Note to You

I want you to know that if you've ever been in a place or with someone and you knew it wasn't right for you, it's okay. That doesn't make you weak or less.

Rebel Rising

Be honest about what you knew before you were able to act. That knowing was strength, not weakness, even if you didn't act right away.

Chapter 15

Wish You a Happy Journey

Dave arranged to come down, and together we rented a moving truck. This time, we weren't starting over with just a few boxes and children in tow. The kids were with my mom and dad back in Ohio, and it was just the two of us packing up the house, loading the truck, and knowing this move was different.

The night before we left, we picked up Chinese food for dinner. I opened my fortune cookie, and it read, *"Wish you a happy journey."* It felt prophetic. I took a photo of the sunset that evening, it hung right behind the moving truck, and for a moment, I felt like it was God's way of telling me this was the right move to make.

We decided to leave early the next morning, around 5:00 a.m. It was scorching hot, one of the hottest days of summer in South Carolina. It was the very end of July, and I remember this overwhelming sense of fear washing over me. I was leaving our home, our keys, our garage remotes, and once that door closed, there was no going back.

As we pulled out of the driveway, I knew it was the last time I'd ever close that door. When we drove through the gates of our neighborhood, I knew it was the last time I'd ever leave them. Panic set in that I can't even fully describe. My heart dropped straight into my stomach, and as we drove away, tears streamed down my face.

My closest friend didn't even say goodbye. She avoided me completely. I felt like I was losing everything I'd worked so hard for; everything I'd believed would finally be stability.

I had found another job back home at a small TV station, making only a fraction of what I'd been earning before. I'd also found a house for us to live in and enrolled the kids back in their old school. It was as if the past ten months had been erased, but the impact of those months, everything they took and taught me, would never leave. I would never be the same. Nothing would ever be the same.

I started working at the new TV station, and Dave went back to his old lawn care company. I quickly realized how much I hated the job. The station was farther from home, and even though my sales territory was close to my house, my manager didn't want me to work out of the satellite office near me. She wanted me to drive forty minutes to the main office every day.

She was younger than me, far less experienced, and a complete micromanager. She didn't trust my judgment on commercials, didn't want to assign me accounts, and questioned almost everything I did. To make matters worse, this station was a direct competitor to the one I had come from, and not a very good one. The entire environment felt off from the moment I got there.

One afternoon, I received a call from my mom that my grandfather had suffered a stroke. I left the satellite office immediately and headed to her house, which was in a very rural area with almost no cell service.

My manager had already called and left a voicemail before I arrived, but while I was at my mom's, she called again. The call didn't come through because I had no signal, so it went straight to voicemail.

When I finally listened to it, she was furious, threatening me for not answering, even after I explained it was a family emergency. That was my breaking point. I knew right then this wasn't the place for me, and I quit my job.

A couple of months later I received devastating and unexpected news. My childhood friend Bryan passed away.

If you've ever lost a friend, especially one you had known for a long time, and one that you shared many important life moments with, you will understand then all the feelings I had. Great sadness, mixed with guilt. We never had a chance to catch up after that phone call a year earlier. I had moved and life got in the way. Or maybe, I just didn't try hard enough. Either way, I was completely devastated.

As I was reeling with that loss, I didn't receive any comfort from my husband. No sympathy for how much I hurt.

I feel extremely depressed. Dave was off work for the winter. Being around him felt like a giant weight, instead of a weight being lifted. Not being independent with my own career and salary was extremely hard on me.

However, I tried to take comfort that this was giving me quality time with my daughter that I hadn't had since she was an infant.

I spent the next five months trying to find a new job, but where we lived, it was incredibly difficult. I finally landed something, but it was severely underpaid compared to what I was used to.

Honestly, it was almost the same wage I'd made right out of high school. Still, I knew it could be temporary. I saw potential growth inside the company, so I took the chance and accepted the job.

Meanwhile, my marriage continued to fall apart. Things at home were volatile. I wasn't happy. The kids weren't happy, and I told Dave that.

Dave's job was seasonal, but when the season returned, he decided, once again, that he didn't want to go back. I wasn't making enough to carry the full weight of our family, and the stress was crushing. Dave also started acting strangely.

When I came home from work, he would be anxious and eager to leave the house. He began hanging around our neighbor, running errands with him, which made no sense, because the neighbor didn't even have a job. What errands could they possibly be running?

Over Memorial Day weekend, I went to my parents for a cookout. Dave didn't want to come. I ended up leaving early with my daughter, keeping the boys at my parents' house. When I walked into our home and headed into my daughter's room, I noticed her window cracked open.

That's when I heard Dave outside, laughing and talking with the neighbor.

He didn't know I was home.

I heard him joke that his "old lady" was suspicious he was doing drugs because she (meaning me) had said his jaw had been moving strangely the other night, going side-to-side quickly, fast, almost cartoonish. The second I heard him confirm it, my stomach dropped.

The only time I'd ever heard of that happening was when someone was on drugs, they refer to it as "cocaine jaw".

I didn't say a word. I grabbed my daughter's shoes, scooped her up, and rushed to the car. As I was strapping her into the car seat, Dave came running around the corner.

"Janice, where are you going? What are you doing?"

I told him he needed to get the hell out. I was done. This was the end of our marriage.

I drove straight back to my parents' house. I stayed there for a week until he finally moved out, and I began the paperwork.

I couldn't afford the house we were living in on my own, and our lease was ending. I didn't know what I was going to do. I prayed over it constantly. I had started packing, assuming the kids, and I would have to move in with my parents. The date was approaching fast.

And then, just like that, God opened a door or should I say a house. A house became available right across the street. Half the price. The perfect size for me and the kids.

Once again, God didn't disappoint.
He didn't fail me.
He delivered right on time.

The house had come through, but my job was coming to an end.

The property I'd been assigned to was owned by an international commercial real estate company. Their whole model was to take failing properties, especially those pending sale, make them profitable, and then sell them.

The property sold, and the new owner wasn't keeping the staff. That especially included marketing.

My only option would have been to stay with the company and relocate, which I did not want to do.

My divorce had just finalized and having just moved into a new home and having recently moved back after trying to relocate before, I knew relocating again wasn't realistic for me or my kids.

I didn't know what I was going to do. I was worried, stressed, and praying for direction.

Then, out of nowhere, I received a call from my former digital manager. She told me a company had reached out to her about a position, but she didn't want it because it was too far for her.

She said she immediately thought of me, that it would be a perfect fit.

I was shocked, honored, and completely caught off guard. This wasn't even on my radar.

I interviewed with the digital director, Jake. He was kind, professional, educated, and immediately impressed with my background. He also pointed out that I lived in the perfect location for the job. After the interview, he asked if I could meet in person for a second one.

A couple of weeks later, I was offered the job. Finally, I was going to be making the kind of salary I needed again.

This was exactly what I had been praying for, the chance for the kids and me to get back on our feet. It felt like freedom. I had a beautiful little home that was ours. I started the new job, and I loved it. I didn't even mind the driving.

Every morning, I'd take my two youngest kids to daycare so they could catch the bus to school. It wasn't far from the house, but there were days it was a struggle to get the kids ready and there on time to make my hour drive to the office. If there were days when the kids were sick, and I couldn't be there, my mom or her friend helped care for them, which was immensely helpful.

For a moment, everything felt settled.

One day I was on Facebook and received a friend request. You won't believe who it was from! Damon! Yes, that Damon, the one from high school. I hadn't seen him since the night 14 years earlier where he stood me up. I wondered what he'd been up to. I clicked accept.

Reflection

Turning the Page

There are moments when you must walk away from something familiar, even when you want it to work. Letting go can feel heavy and unfair. But release is sometimes the first honest step toward peace. Strength isn't measured by how tightly you hold on. It's measured by the courage it takes to choose what's right for you.

A Note to You

Choosing a new direction isn't failure. It's faith. Sometimes God closes a door because what's behind it can't hold who you're becoming. Trust the shift, even when it's uncomfortable.

Rebel Rising

What are you ready to let go of, and what do you want to make room for?

Chapter 16

Doors 1 or 2?

About a week had passed since I accepted Damon's friend request on Facebook. He hadn't reached out, and I wasn't planning to message him either. From his profile, I could see he had several kids, maybe as many as I did, and it didn't look like he was in a relationship. He didn't list a job, but he had posted a couple of videos of himself welding. The rest of his posts were mostly political.

One afternoon I posted a selfie, and a few hours later I noticed a heart reaction from Damon. Not long after that, he sent me a message through Facebook Messenger. It was something simple, something like, "Hey, how've you been? It's been a long time. You look great!"

My mind started racing. How do I respond? Is he flirting? Or is this just a friendly message after all these years?

I wrote back with something like, "I'm doing great, thank you. That's sweet of you. How have you been?"

His reply came quickly. He said, "Yeah, I always thought you were really pretty. I had a crush on you."

I was surprised. "Really? I had no idea."

We kept chatting for a while. At one point, he asked if I wanted to meet up with him when he got back into town. He said he was working at a plant in northern Ohio doing welding on their pork rind machines.

I told him sure; it would be good to catch up after so many years.

He asked if I was single, and I told him I had just gotten divorced a few months earlier. I asked him the same question, and he said he was single too.

A few weeks went by, and we continued talking while he was still working out of town. He told me he hated it there, said the whole plant smelled like rotten flesh, but the pay was good. That is when I learned he was what they call a traveling welder. He specialized in food and beverage welding and helped put together breweries and other food manufacturing facilities. From the way he described it, he seemed to do very well financially and was skilled at what he did.

Over those weeks, we grew more comfortable with each other, and the conversations became flirtatious. He asked for pictures of me and would go on about how hot I was and how he couldn't wait to see me in person again. He told me I had hardly aged. He let me know he would be coming home on a short break before returning to finish the job, and we made plans to have lunch at one of my favorite Japanese restaurants in town.

I arrived a little early in my Toyota Sienna minivan. A few minutes later, I watched Damon pull in driving a very old Chevy Express van. For someone who claimed to be doing very well financially, I couldn't understand why he was driving something that looked twenty years old and as if it had lived a very hard life.

I got out of my minivan and waited for him to get out of his. He had short dark brown hair and was wearing a beige hat, black framed glasses, khaki wranglers, and a shirt with a button up shirt over it that was halfway buttoned with cowboy work boots. He gave me an awkward hug and looked down at my cleavage and immediately commented on how he appreciated the glow they gave off. I had put on some sort of shimmery lotion that day.

We went inside the restaurant and were seated by a nice waitress who immediately recognized him from when we all had gone to high school. I had no idea who she was, but she made sure to comment about recognizing him. The Rottenburg family was very well known since Damon's dad was a small politician and was at one time our county commissioner, making him popular when we were in high school together.

We ordered our food, and Damon began to talk. In fact, that's all he did. He didn't listen. The moment I started to speak, he would start to speak. It was very off putting, and I wasn't really feeling things like I had hoped I would. It didn't feel like he had really matured a whole lot. He told me about the kids and how he had custody of four of them because their mom was a "worthless junkie", his words, not mine. I was also really surprised to find out that they had just had another baby together. He said it was a mistake and he was really upset by it, but he was adamant that he was not with her. He hated her. He also said that she was staying at his house with all the kids since he was out of town working; it made the most sense. She didn't work. I was really trying to process all this information and had a lot of questions, but I didn't feel like diving into it at that moment.

It was time to leave and out of nowhere he told me he would follow me. I said, "Follow me where?" He said, "Your house of course." I couldn't believe what I was hearing. What exactly was he thinking? But I begrudgingly said, "Okay. I have a couple of hours before the kids get home from school." Honestly, I wasn't entirely sure what he meant about coming over to my house. I thought perhaps he wanted to keep talking. I see my naivety now.

Damon returned to work a few days later, and his communication with me became less and less. I wasn't sure what to make of it. Either he was genuinely busy or he had gotten what he wanted and was done.

After a week of not hearing from him, I sent a message that said, "I really enjoyed our time together, but I think it's best we just stay friends."

Almost immediately, messages started pouring in.
"What?"
"Why?"
"WTF?"

They kept coming.
Eventually he texted that he didn't want

to "just stay friends" and wanted to know why I felt that way. I told him his lack of consistency made it clear he wasn't interested in the same thing I was, and while I enjoyed the time we had, I wasn't going to waste mine.

Through the conversation, I learned he was home now. The job had wrapped up, and he needed to come into town to pick up some items he had in layaway at a sporting goods store near me. He asked me to meet with him.

When we met, he kissed me — awkwardly — and then insisted we go get ice cream down the street. We talked for a while before he asked if I would go with him to the sports store next door.

The moment we walked in, it was clear they knew him well. The store was lined with guns, ammunition, and tactical gear. Damon had served briefly in the Army and had a strong love for guns. He ordered a tripod, which they explained would take about a week to come in.

We left and said goodbye without defining anything about what this was between us. It was obvious Damon was uncomfortable talking about feelings. He shut down any time I tried, so I let it go.

Later that night, he texted me asking if he could come over. I told him he would need to wait until my kids were asleep because I wasn't bringing him around them. Not yet.

He came over for a few hours, and when it was time for him to leave, he grew irritated about going home because his "baby mom," as he called her, was still staying there. He went on and on about how much he hated her, how lazy she was, how disgusting she was, how he wanted her out. He ranted for a long time before finally leaving.

The next day, Damon texted me saying he had kicked her out and sent her to live with her mom. She took the baby with her, and he kept the four kids he had custody of. He had an older son as well, but that child lived with his mother out of town.

He started sending me photos of his house, especially the kitchen, and it was a complete disaster. He kept talking about how clean my house was and how much he admired that. As someone who considers herself to be OCD, the sight of what he sent was overwhelming.

He asked if I would come over and help him get it cleaned up.

I was working full time, traveling long distances every day, and had my own house and kids to take care of. Cleaning another grown adult's home was the last thing I wanted to do. But he begged. He said he didn't have anyone else. He even suggested I bring my kids and let them play with his, but I wasn't ready for that at all.

He lived just a street over from my parents, so I told him I would see if they could watch my kids for a little while, and I would come help him.

When Damon talked about his house, I did not picture what I saw when I pulled up. The house sat on a hill in a strange layout. Instead of entering at the bottom where you parked, you had to walk up large paver stones to get to the front porch, which wrapped around the house and overlooked a small pond. There was nothing around but land, cows, and his parents' home next door, within viewing range but at least an acre away. Other neighbors were at the top of the hill, far enough away that no one would hear anything.

When I walked inside, there was not a clear pathway in sight.

The kitchen counters were piled high. Dried food coated the cabinets, refrigerator, and dishwasher.
An old wooden dining table sat against the kitchen windows, buried in clutter. The small island was covered in random objects.

He told me he didn't know where to begin, and that there were cleaning supplies under the sink. His kids ran around the house chaotically — ages four, six, seven, and nine — and based on the kitchen alone, I could only imagine what the rest of the house looked like.

I started cleaning the kitchen. To my disappointment, Damon didn't help. He sat in a chair at the table watching me and played on his phone.

I finally said something, and he got up briefly to shuffle through some papers before calling his seven-year-old daughter over to help because *he* felt annoyed and overwhelmed.

I went home that night knowing, without a doubt, that I did not ever want to go back there to clean that man's house again.

About a week went by, and Damon asked if my kids and I wanted to go to a train festival with his kids. He said his dad was one of the organizers and that it would be fun for the kids and a great way for them all to meet. We had been seeing each other for about four months, so I figured it would be fine.

We went, and we all had a blast. The kids got along really well and were close in age. My daughter loved playing with his two girls, especially the youngest, since they were the same age. Later that night, his kids begged him to stay over at our house. He looked at me and asked if it was okay. Being put on the spot, I didn't feel like I could say no, so they stayed.

That became a regular occurrence. One day, to my surprise, Damon showed up with a huge bag of their laundry.

He claimed their dryer had quit working and asked if they could use mine. You can imagine how much laundry came with five kids. He made his children load the washer and dryer while he sat on the couch. The kids and I folded everything together and loaded it into baskets for them to take home.

Whenever his kids misbehaved, he would flick them in the head or threaten them. It never sat well with me, and I often found myself stepping in. He never crossed that line with my kids. I made it very clear from the beginning that I would not tolerate that.

Before I knew it, we were always together as a "family" unit. Either we were staying at his house, or he was staying at mine. My lease was coming up for renewal, and

Damon said, "We're together all the time anyway. Why don't you move in with me? Think of all the money you will save." I still had a couple of months to decide, but financially it made sense. He did not have rent or a mortgage payment, and we were already together constantly. Still, it was something I needed to think about. We had not even said we loved each other.

One day, while at Damon's house, I took a selfie wearing his hoodie. When I went home, I posted a picture on Facebook. I didn't tag him or mention him. He never talked about our relationship online, updated his status, or posted anything about being with me.

A short while later, I received a message from Damon about the photo. He was furious. I couldn't believe what I was reading. He completely lost it! He sent message after message, saying things that were cruel and completely out of character from how he had been with me. I was blindsided. He had never acted that way before.

I was sitting in the waiting area at the auto shop getting new tires put on when he tried to call me. When I didn't answer, he got even angrier. I told him I couldn't talk where I was. He demanded that I delete the photo immediately. Exhausted by the outburst and not wanting to deal with the tantrum anymore, I deleted it.

After I left the auto shop, he called me, and suddenly he was calm again. Normal. Like nothing had happened at all.

Just a few nights before, Damon surprised me by opening emotionally. He told me how much he loved and appreciated me, how he saw me for who I was, how amazing and hardworking he thought I was, and how thankful he was that we had reconnected. I remember feeling caught off guard by the sudden tenderness but also touched by it. It felt sincere in that moment.

Right before that meltdown, I had already told my landlord that I would not be renewing my lease.

Now I wasn't so sure.

I'll never forget my mom coming over to my house. We sat in my living room, and she said to me "Janice, are you sure you want to move in with him." I told her I wasn't. After going through the ordeal with my now second ex-husband, I was afraid to be in another situation that was turbulent. I enjoyed the peace I had created in my new home, new space, and new job. But I felt a real connection to Damon and his kids.

Things had been better with Damon. He hadn't acted out toward me in any negative way. He was getting stressed though because he didn't have any work coming in and the most he had since we started dating when he returned from the pork rind plant was a weekend job a few hours away, and they terminated him pretty quickly.

He really surprised me one day when I was over at his house, and he was on the phone with an old friend who had an e-commerce business. The friend was struggling to keep sales coming in, and

Damon told him how his "girlfriend," meaning me, worked for Google.
First, I was shocked that he referred me as his girlfriend.
Second, I did not work for Google. I worked for a Google certified company. A very big difference.

Still, I wasn't sure what to do. I was perplexed because of Jekyll and Hyde behavior. He wasn't working now, but he assured me it was temporary and that if he had a truck, it would be much easier.

So, I took out a personal loan, we found a truck and drove up to get it.
When it came time to do the title during the sale, the owner of the very small and shady looking dealership kept insisting my name be put on it.

After all, it was my personal loan, and I was the one handing over the cash. The bad part was that the truck needed work.

I told my landlord I was reconsidering renewing my lease. I had about a month left before it expired. I wanted time to really sit with the decision. It felt like being offered Door 1 or Door 2 in a game show.

Door 1: everything I had worked on building.
Door 2: something I couldn't fully picture but felt pressured toward anyway.

I had spoken to Damon about my fear of having 8 children in his 3-bedroom house. How exactly was that going to work? He told me that the large room in the front of the house that they were currently using as a "playroom" for the kids, which was quite large, would be perfect for the 3 boys, and we could put the 3 girls in a room. It was like we were the Brady Bunch. He told me, I would have to clean the front room though if that's where I wanted them to be. It seemed feasible. Plus, we would be closer to my parents, and I really liked that idea.

On top of everything, I had my little dog, and Damon didn't believe dogs should be allowed inside. That meant I would have to rehome her. My work schedule made things difficult anyway, so part of me rationalized it. But it still hurt.

The answer came as a knock on my door one afternoon. I opened it to find my landlord standing there. He needed an answer, and he needed it fast. He had other tenants lined up, and they were willing to pay more. He could not risk waiting on me.

We were moving. Again.

Reflection

Clear Confusion

There are times when someone's behavior leaves you feeling unsteady, unsure, or emotionally tangled. One moment feels warm, the next cold. One conversation feels promising, the next unsettling. When people switch masks quickly, it creates confusion and confusion is not clarity; it is a warning.

A Note to You

When your spirit hesitates, it is trying to protect you. God is not the author of chaos. The right path will not require you to silence your needs or shrink your peace.

Rebel Rising

Notice one moment where things felt confusing instead of calm. Write what your body knew before your mind tried to explain it away.

Chapter 17

Hell of a Ride

Moving day arrived quicker than I was ready for. I had to re-home my dog, register the kids in a new school, work, and pack. Damon had completely underestimated how much stuff I had.

He also didn't do much to prepare for us to move into his house. The washer and dryer in his tiny laundry room were still there, even though mine needed to go in. I had a couch and loveseat, he had a worn-out sectional, and he hadn't gotten rid of it. I figured we would just move everything in and sort it out later, once we were settled.

Damon had his best friend, Chucky, and sister Valerie, come help pack everything up. His sister and I had known each other back in high school and she had it pretty rough since then. She had a rap sheet about a mile long, struggled with drug addiction, and had lost custody of her first son to her parents and recently had another baby who was being raised by her parents while she continued to struggle with her sobriety since his father had ended his own life when she was pregnant. I was really surprised when she wanted to help with the move. She never really seemed to like me. Maybe it's because for a brief time I had dated her ex-boyfriend, but that was 15 years ago or so.

In the middle of moving, she needed to go to the pharmacy to grab a prescription for her son. We had to take her because she had a suspended license.

While we were on the way there, she began to ask Damon and I a bunch of questions about moving in together, one being, "Do you even love each other?"

Damon replied snarky back to her "You know I'm not capable of love." I knew he loved me. He had said it privately.

I knew he was also not one to open up emotionally, especially not to her, so I wasn't surprised by his comment. He grabbed my hand and gave it a little gentle squeeze and a sheepish smile.

Valerie shot back, "Well when Nathan was alive, we couldn't stop loving each other. Couldn't stand being apart."

Damon didn't miss a beat. "Yeah, well he also pimped you out in Mexico and then ended his life while you were pregnant with his kid."

Valerie went quiet, sinking back into her seat. I felt horrible for her.

We pulled back into my driveway, and Chucky had been loading Damon's van and the small trailer with our things. It took the entire day and several trips. By the time we finished, it was late and we were exhausted.

I loaded the kids into my van, and we prepared to leave. Because the trailer didn't have working lights, I had to follow directly behind Damon. He chose the back way home, so there was less chance of running into any cops who might pull him over.

The road was a pitch-black country road, not a single streetlight in sight. It was unpaved, full of ruts, gravel, and dips that shook the van with every mile. All I could see were Damon's taillights bouncing in the distance, guiding me down a road I wasn't even sure I wanted to be on.

I was relieved when we had finally arrived at the house, it had been a long day.

I wanted to get settled right away. I needed order, familiar things, and a sense of home. But Damon pushed back on everything. He had a cheap metal platform bed with a queen mattress, and I had my king-sized tufted sleigh bed — the one thing I was excited to sleep on after such a long, exhausting move. I thought we would set it up immediately.

Instead, to my shock, he refused to take down his bed. He just set my king mattress on top of his queen frame like it was nothing. It looked ridiculous, unstable, and completely wrong.

All of my shoes — enough to fill a large black trash bag — were shoved into a corner by the dresser. My furniture, brand new and something I had worked hard for, was stacked in the front room that used to be the kids' playroom. All my boxes were piled there too. He wouldn't unpack a single thing. He wouldn't even let me.

I couldn't understand it. Why move me and my kids into this house if nothing of ours was allowed to exist in it? Why bring us here only to push us into corners and piles?

His furniture was old and worn. Mine was nice. But none of it mattered to him.

My daughter and his two girls were suddenly sharing a queen-sized bed, when she had always had her own. And we had four boys squeezed into one room — two sharing a bed and two sleeping on mattresses on the floor.

Nothing about it felt right.
Nothing felt like home.
It was not the situation I thought I was walking into.

A few days later, while the kids were away and it was just us, I was lying on his stomach. He didn't like me to lay up on his chest and kept his phone close to his face.

I had moved a certain way that hurt him by mistake, and without a thought, he elbowed me on the top of my head very hard. I was shocked! I didn't know what to say. I just got up and left the room. I didn't want him to see how much it had hurt me. Not just physically but emotionally.

Tears welled in my eyes. I waited a few minutes before I returned. I said calmly, "I don't know what that was or why you did that, but don't do that again."

He apologized profusely. Claiming it was a knee jerk reaction. It sure didn't feel like it to me.

One night, while Damon was out, I couldn't stand looking at my boys squeezing into that tiny room anymore. They deserved better. They deserved space. So, the kids and I moved things around in the front room and set up their bunk beds. They were so excited to finally have beds again. They were relieved. They felt settled, even if only a little.

But when Damon came home, everything changed.

The moment he saw the beds, he exploded.

He started screaming at me, red-faced, shaking with anger, and before I could process what was happening, he charged toward me, in front of all the kids.

Instinct took over.

I grabbed the first thing within reach, a belt that had been lying nearby, swung it, hit the wall behind him, and yelled for him to stay away from me and my children.

Everything went still.
Silent.
Heavy.

That night, something shifted.
And nothing felt safe anymore.

Reflection

Flicker of Truth

Sometimes the strongest part of you isn't the voice that fights. It's the quiet feeling that whispers, something is off. You might not have the full story yet, and you might not feel ready to make a change. But that first flicker matters. It's often the earliest sign that your peace is trying to protect you.

A Note to You

If your spirit hesitated, there was a reason. You don't have to explain it perfectly for it to be real.

Rebel Rising

What's one early sign you'll trust faster next time, and why?

Chapter 18

Disappointment

The weeks went by, and he still wasn't
working. Everything in the house was
still packed and crowded. My washer sat
wrapped up on the porch, while my
dryer was being used, and for some
reason he just wouldn't replace the
washing machine. Christmas was coming
fast, and taking care of all of us
financially was putting real strain on me.
I had moved in thinking we would have
more, not less. Money was so tight that I
had to take a loan from my 401(k) just to
buy Christmas presents.

One day I went out to buy gifts for the
kids while mine was with my parents and
his children were with their mom.
Damon didn't go with me. He said his
dad had something he needed to do.
When I got home, the van was filled with
gifts. I was surprised to find him lying on

the couch, glued to his phone. I asked him to help me bring everything inside, but he just laid there. So, I carried all of it up the hill and into the house by myself. I started wrapping presents, and he stayed on his phone the entire time.

A few days later, while he was gone, I couldn't shake how suspicious things had started to feel. He still hadn't acknowledged me as his girlfriend on social media. Anytime I tagged him, he removed it immediately. His relationship status was still set to single. And he guarded his phone like it was the most valuable thing he owned. It slept under his pillow. He kept it in his hand constantly. I wasn't even allowed to lay on his chest where I might see it.

While I didn't have access to his phone, he did have a laptop. And I was savvy enough to figure out the password. When I logged in and opened his browser, to my shock he was still logged into Facebook.

That's when I found it.

Three different women he was talking to behind my back.

One he was trying to meet at a hotel the same day I had come home from work early.

The room started to turn black around me.

My hands went numb.
My heart was pounding so hard I could feel the vein in my neck pulsing.

I was horrified.

I had just moved in with him.
I was taking care of his kids.
I was taking care of him financially.
And this is what he called love?

I called my mom and told her I was moving out and what I had found. She said I could stay with them for a few days, but that was all she could do.

I called Damon to ask where he was. I
wasn't going to tell him over the phone. I
drove to him so I could confront him in
person. He happened to be with his dad.
I got out of the car and laid into him,
telling him I was leaving.

He begged me not to.
He asked me to come back to the house
so we could talk.
I told him there was nothing to talk
about.
He insisted.
So I went with him.

He swore nothing had happened.
To me, it was cheating.
He begged me not to leave. He told me
he loved me, that he needed me, that it
would never happen again.

And I believed him.

I called my mom and canceled our
move.

Christmas came quickly, and it was also his birthday. He loved cheesecake, so I bought the perfect one and planned to bring it out at the end of the night with a candle lit for him.

He had taken his kids down to their moms for Christmas. On his way home, he called me and said he was stopping at the bar near our house. I was surprised and disappointed that it was even open. I had been looking forward to a cozy evening together for our first Christmas and his birthday. He told me he wouldn't be long.

He lied.

I waited until one in the morning, sitting alone by the fire while my kids slept peacefully in the other room. Eventually, I gave up and went to bed.

Valentine's Day came, and once we had a kid-free night. Damon wanted to go down to a friend's bar that had just opened, and I was excited to go somewhere new. To my surprise, several of my friends were there, and it ended up being a fun night. I hadn't cut loose like that in a long time, and I mistakenly drank more than I should have.

I thought we were heading home afterward, but Damon decided we needed to stop at the bar closest to our house. I barely remember walking into it or getting out of it.

The next morning, I started vomiting. And vomiting. And vomiting. I couldn't stop. It was the worst I had ever been sick in my life. At first, Damon was actually sweet. He came into the bathroom and held me while I got sick, but after twenty rounds of throwing up, I called my mom. She insisted that I see a doctor immediately.

Damon didn't think I needed to go at first, but when I couldn't stop getting sick, he finally agreed to take me. The nearest hospital was about twenty-five minutes away.

I got in the car, buckled up, and held a bag in my lap in case I got sick again. That's when he told me he wanted to make a pit stop first. There was a store he wanted to go to because he needed hops for the homemade beer, he had suddenly decided to start brewing.

He had this bright idea that he would open his own brewery one day.

The issue was that the store wasn't anywhere near the hospital. It was in the opposite direction. In another state. Almost an hour away.

He told me that after we went there, he would take me to the hospital.

When we finally arrived at the hospital, my vitals were not good. I was severely dehydrated and still vomiting nonstop. They immediately started an IV and gave me medication to help stop the nausea. While I was lying there, my mom texted me, worried because she hadn't heard from me in a while. I didn't tell her that he had taken a long detour before taking me to the hospital. I didn't want to worry her or deal with the questions I knew she would have.

The doctors weren't sure if it was alcohol poisoning or if someone had slipped something into my drink. They ran tests and monitored me closely.

All I could do was lie there, drained and scared, trying to make sense of how the night had gone so terribly wrong.

Reflection

When Hope Meets Reality

Disappointment can hit hard when you believed in someone, trusted their words, or stayed because you wanted things to work. When reality doesn't match the hope you had, it can feel personal, even when it isn't. But these moments often carry clarity. They show you what you value, what you expect, and what you're no longer willing to settle for.

A Note to You

Disappointment doesn't mean you were foolish. It means you were open, invested, and hopeful. That's not a flaw. That's the starting point.

Rebel Rising

This is your permission to raise the bar. What are you no longer available for, even if it means someone is disappointed?

____

____

____

____

____

____

____

____

____

____

____

____

____

____

____

Chapter 19

The Last Hurrah

Damon had finally secured a job in Virginia, welding for a dairy plant. I was relieved that he would finally be going back to work, but the only issue was that he needed money to go. He promised he would pay me back with his first paycheck. After all, he would be making fifteen thousand a month.

I had to pay for his lodging until they reimbursed him, tools he needed, special shoes, and some clothes. We now had a shared bank account, so every day I would get notified when he would go and spend fifty dollars on a steak meal. I confronted him and asked him why he felt that it was necessary to do that every day, and he yelled at me about how dare I suggest he didn't deserve to eat well after a hard day at work.

I decided after a couple of weeks that I would make the five-hour drive down to see him and take him some food and other things that would make him stay away from home better. A co-worker agreed to sit with my kids while I went down, and his kids went to visit their mom.

I was very disappointed when I arrived; he wasn't there yet. He made me sit and wait for him for about an hour and when he did arrive, he didn't so much as give me a hug. Just rushed into the hotel room he was staying in, leaving me to carry everything in myself.

He went to take a bath, and I found a receipt with two phone numbers written on it. I asked him about it, and he said they were a couple that worked at the restaurant he had befriended. I didn't press.

The next day when he went to work, I went to the laundry mat to do his laundry. Once his clothes were drying and I was folding them and found a mysterious sock. Odd, I had made sure the dryer was completely empty before I had loaded it. I wondered, was he faithful.

The next month Damon's Dad had received news from a friend of his that owned a home that he was evicting the person who was supposed to be purchasing it on a land contract.

The house, he said, was a perfect size for our size family and on five acres of land with a very large commercial size garage. This particularly excited Damon because he was looking for a place to put up his brewery, and he thought this could be the right location.

The problem was, Damon didn't have any money, but I did. So, they convinced me to purchase it on a land contract.

Unfortunately, Damon's job was shut down with the onslaught of Covid. He had been paid quite well for the six weeks he had worked, but once he received his pay, when I asked him to pay back the three grand it cost me to put him to work, he told me if it meant that much to me, he pointed, there is the door.

I should have known he wouldn't pay me back. His dad had even told me that's why he quit helping put him to work. He never kept the job, was always fired, and never ever paid him back.

Somehow, Damon had convinced his dad that his brewery idea was a good one, and I had found a manufacturing plant that was closing up for auction with just the type of equipment needed for the brewery.

Damon decided to go up on the first day of the auction alone. It went so well that once his dad learned about it, he couldn't say no and went with him, winning a bunch of the equipment.

He had introduced me to a guy I had known in elementary school, Doyle, while at the bar close to our home. I hadn't recognized him at first, I mean it had been thirty years since I had last seen him. Doyle wasn't working, and this made him the perfect henchmen for Damon and his dad.

 They spent the next several weeks loading up the place.

A month after covid had shut down the job Damon was on, his boss called and asked if he and his friend could come pay us a visit. They knew I was in marketing and were launching a business manufacturing THC and mushroom supplements and wanted my insights on how to go about it.

I didn't know how we were going to cram them into our house, but Damon talked to his kids' mom and convinced her to take the kids. This was easier since school was shut down due to covid-19.

I had met Damon's boss, Steve, when we were down in Virginia, but I had never met his friend Josh. Josh was a free spirit. A creative entrepreneur. He was a tad flirty with me, but I ignored it.

Steve also had the opportunity for another job in the area, so he and Damon were working on the blueprints in the kitchen of the new house I had purchased, and while they did that Josh and I would talk about marketing his new venture.

Almost immediately you could see a shift in Damon's demeanor. He was the one who had set this up, so I couldn't understand why he was so upset by it.

Damon had some friends from California with a camper that had nowhere to stay. He and the guy had worked together years prior, so he offered them the land behind the new house to stay until they could find a new home. I wasn't a big fan of them. The wife was unstable, and they both drank too much.

Josh and I had built a good friendship while he was in town, but sadly he and Steve needed to get back home to Virginia. When they were there, I felt so safe. I didn't have to worry about Damon yelling at me and causing arguments.

Watching their truck leave, I felt a huge wave of anxiety and fear.

The next morning, I stopped over at the new house and Damon came walking over to me. I thought he was going to hug me, but instead he said in a low growl "Kat says you've been flirting with Josh." Kat was the wife of his friend.

I was really taken aback. I didn't feel like I had been flirting with Josh. I mean, when we got along and we were spending a lot of time together on the marketing plan, but flirting, no. From there the accusations began to fly. He began to accuse me of cheating on him with him.

This became the turning point and lit the fuse for what was to come.

Reflection

Overfunctioning

When someone else lives in chaos, it has a way of spilling onto you. Not all at once, but slowly. You start adjusting, covering, smoothing things over, carrying more, doing more, explaining more. Then one day you realize you've become the one responsible for problems you didn't create. That kind of pattern doesn't just drain your schedule. It drains your peace.

A Note to You

Your strength is not meant to babysit someone else's dysfunction. You are allowed to step back. You are allowed to let consequences be honest.

Rebel Rising

Name one thing you've been carrying that isn't yours. Write one sentence you can live by going forward: "I'm no longer responsible for ________."

Chapter 20

The Fuse

Things really took a turn after the accusations came flying. Damon became increasingly more volatile. One night as he was still accusing me of cheating on him with Josh, he spit at me from across the room. It was absolutely disgusting.

The arguments and his drinking were so bad that I started to secretly record them on my phone using a voice recorder app. Partially for my own sanity, because he would deny things he said in the moment and this was proof, to myself at least, that they were being said.

He became very comfortable calling me horrific names like c**t, and any other way he could put me down. One night he insisted we go to the bar so he could shoot pool with Doyle. I loved shooting pool as well and was looking for a reprieve. Typically, if I gave in to what he wanted to do it would improve his mood. But that night didn't happen.

When we went to the bar, I ended up shooting pool with Doyle which made Damon furious. Only he was to shoot pool with him. On the way home he started screaming at me, cursing, calling me names.

When I yelled back, he stopped the truck in the middle of the road. It was terrifying. We were in the middle of nowhere. Not a person in sight. He told me if I didn't shut my mouth he would shut it for me.

I had had enough. I began thinking about how I could leave, now that I had another house. It needed some work, but I could live there while we worked on it. I had to get out of this situation. It was becoming very scary.

It started to become physical in ways that I didn't realize at that time they were abusive.

For instance, when we were intimate, which at this point, I felt I was obligated to appease him, he would bite my upper arm so hard, it would leave large bruises. On day his dad had commented on it. He chastized him for it, and Damon blew it off. After that he started doing it to my back, this way it wouldn't be seen.

I knew I needed to do my best to appease him while I figured out how I could leave. At the same time, I was very attached to his children, especially his youngest daughter.

I'll never forget one day after we had an argument we had to leave to go somewhere, she stood there with her fine blonde hair messy hanging around her face, and her little glasses, tears welled in her eyes, her tiny fists balled up, "I don't want you to leave!".

My heart sank. I loved her like my own daughter. What would happen to her if I left. Leaving meant I would never see her again. I wanted so desperately to fix our relationship.

Damon started hanging out with Doyle a lot more. They would always be working on a piece of equipment, since he was a mechanic, and Damon's dad had quite a few things that needed work done. You could tell that Doyle was starting to see the mistreatment taking place. He was married with three small children of his own. His wife was a crack addict, currently recovering. They were an odd match.

He was rather quiet, worked hard, and kept to himself. She was loud, had a bad temper, and was much younger than him. One day he called and asked if we could loan them some money for food. I told him I would be more than happy to pay her to come over and clean the house, so she did. After that, they would come over to hang out from time to time.

Another month went by, and Damon finally got work at a local popsicle plant that was updating their pipe equipment. I was hopeful that returning to work would alleviate some of the tension between us. Instead, it created more distance. He would tell me he was going out with the guys after work, but I was never allowed to go.

One evening he went out for hours, wouldn't respond to my text or phone calls, and when he came home, he immediately ran to the bathroom.

A couple weeks later, the day before Father's Day. I had gone to the store and gotten him a card for the kids to give him on Father's Day morning. I hoped that he and I would get some time alone together, maybe go to dinner or something.

That evening he told me that he had to go run an errand and that when he came back maybe he and I could go to the bar close to our house.

So, I went home and fed the kids. I did some house chores. Took a bath. When I received a text message from Doyle's wife. She asked if I wanted to hang out since Damon and Doyle were going to the bar to shoot pool.

It became very clear; Damon never had any intention of spending time with me that evening. I tried to call him, but he kept rejecting me.

I sent him a text, no answer. I wasn't having it. So, I got ready. My thirteen-year-old son, the oldest in the house, could babysit and had done so on many occasions.

Only two of Damon's kids were at home, the older two, and I was only going to be a mile down the road. I told my son where I was going, I wouldn't be long, and to call if he needed anything.

When I walked in the bar and Damon laid eyes on me, you could immediately see the fury behind them that I was there. I walked over to him, smiled, and said "Hey!" "I tried calling you, but you didn't answer. I had a feeling you may be here."

Doyle was shooting pool and came over to take a shot, said hello, and talked with me for a minute before going back. Damon was giving me silent treatment.

The bartender, Pam, a "friend" of ours, was dressed differently than usual. She had long dreads and typically wore jeans or leggings, but not tonight, tonight she had on booty shorts.

Damon needed another drink and helped himself to the fridge nearby. Tired of his silent treatment, I went and sat down a few seats away from him.

There was a girl near me who was young, blonde and pretty. She was tipsy and was hanging out with her friend who was trying to cheer her up over her recent breakup. She and I started talking about men and how difficult they could be. I said "Yeah, that's my boyfriend down there." My eyes shifted to the left. "He's mad I showed up tonight. He doesn't want me here." Within a few minutes I started receiving messages from him.

"Why are you here?"

"Do you know how stupid you look right now?"

"You don't need to be talking to that girl."

On and on, they went. Meanwhile, he stood there, glaring at me. It was ridiculous. Why send these to me and not just come over and talk to me.

So, I went over to him again. "You don't need to do that. I'm right here. Why are you saying I look stupid?" He wouldn't answer.

I had had my second drink; Pam had just poured me a third that I didn't want. I said to him that we needed to go home and talk. He agreed but said he had to take Doyle home first. I went out to my minivan and watched him walk out of the bar and into the truck. He hadn't started it yet when I left.

I went home expecting him to be behind me rather momentarily, but he did not show up.

An hour went by. Then two. Then three. Still no Damon. No text. No Call. Nothing. I began to worry.

He had been drinking quite a bit. What if he wrecked.

I texted Doyle's wife and she said that Doyle wasn't home yet.

Another hour passed. She texted and said Doyle was home; she must not have heard the truck when Damon brought him.

I sent another text to Damon. Where are you? I'm worried. This time he responded that he was fine and would be home soon.

He was still mad.

I was hot. Our AC was out. So, I took my clothes off to try to cool off and had my fan on high.

I was tired but before I fell asleep, I thought I had better turn on my voice recorder on my phone, in case he came home and started arguing with me.

The kids were all asleep in their rooms. The girls' room was around the corner from our master bedroom, just on the other side of our master bathroom.

His boys across from the girls' room, and my boys were in the front room at the front of the house.

I took my glasses off and with my phone, put them under my pillow. I'm

extremely near-sighted, so much so that
I can't see them when I take them off, so
I keep them there to grab easily.

My eyes grew heavy as the ceiling fan
was ticking me to sleep.

Content Note

The following chapter contains references to physical violence and assault.

Please take care as you read and pause if you need to.

Chapter 21

June 21, 2020

Father's Day Night

I was awoken briefly by the roar of his truck pulling into the yard beside the house, but I must have drifted right back into sleep. Then I heard it —
"Janice. Janice. Janice."
A whisper, but an angry one.

"Hmmm," I moaned, half asleep.

It was Damon.

"My ex treats me better than you do."

"When I was sick, she took care of me."

"When my back hurts she rubs it for me."

I shot back, "Good. She can have you. I'm moving out tomorrow."

"Get out of my fucking bed." He snapped at me.

"This is my fucking bed. I'm not going anywhere."

Before I could process what was happening, my body began to roll toward the wall where the bag of shoes was.

Damon was lifting my mattress to remove me from the bed.

I stood up. I felt my foot get cut on something I was standing on.

He kept shoving the mattress into me, slamming it, and me, into the wall repeatedly.

I was naked.
I was blind without my glasses.

I was in complete and utter shock.

All I could think was that I had to make him stop.

I pushed back against the mattress. I'm not sure if I managed to force it down or if Damon finally let it drop.

Either way, it fell at a slant, pressed nearly against the wall, and I had to step up onto it to move.

The second I did, Damon lunged.
He jumped onto the mattress with me.

I bent down, desperate to find my glasses
so I could at least *see* what was
happening.

That's when Damon grabbed me by the
throat.

The mattress was leaning and not stable
on top of the queen mattress that lay
under it.

When he grabbed my throat, the
imbalance sent me backwards.

I slammed my head against the
hardwood floor as he began to strangle
me.

At first, I tried to strangle him back, in
defense. I couldn't wrap my hand
around his neck, and this made him
squeeze even more.

I was struggling to breathe.

My left arm was pinned under his leg.

I smacked him across the face a few
times, thinking this would make him let
go.

He squeezed harder.

I couldn't breathe. I could feel him crushing my windpipe.

Finally, I got my other hand free.

My brother, a marine, had taught me in defense to always go for the eyes.

Damon's face was close to mine - his eyes-only inches away.

So, I dug both of my thumbs in them as hard as I could.

This made him stop.

I gasped for air and yelled at him. "You piece of shit! I should have known everything people had said about you was true. I'm done. We're done. I'm leaving tomorrow."

He spit on me.

Then came the first blow.

A sharp crack against my face.

Shock shot through me—*Did he just punch me?*

Another blow.

This time I felt my jaw shift out of place.

Another blow.

A shattering pain just above my cheekbone.

Another.
The room blurred.
Darkness edged in.

I'm not sure if I lost consciousness. I think I did.

Then he stopped. I don't know why—he just... stopped.

I couldn't open my left eye.

Somehow, I was able to get out from under him. I ran toward the mattress. I needed my phone. I needed help. I was badly hurt. I couldn't see it. I rushed up and over the mattress. My phone wasn't there. It must have fallen under the bed. I reached under the top corner of the bed and found it. As soon as I pulled it out, he ripped it out of my hands.

Not able to see, I couldn't grab it from him.

Blood filled my mouth. It pooled. I spit into the sink and looked into the mirror.

It was horror.

My left eye swollen shut.
A long scratch down my cheek—his
fingernail.

My face bloodied, swollen, red.

My lip split.
The entire left side was obliterated.

Damon came rushing into the bathroom
as I was wrapping a towel around myself.

He looked at my face and said "Oh my
God, Janice. I'm going to jail for Father's
Day, aren't I?"

"Yes, you are!" I said

I ran for the bedroom door. He came
right behind me and forced it shut. I
tried to open it again. Again, he shut it.
The next time I tried to yell for my
oldest son to help me.

Again, Damon shut it, all while holding
my phone.

I elbowed him hard in the ribs, grabbed
my phone, ripped the door open, and
ran for the front door.

I tried calling 911. It wouldn't go through.

We lived in the middle of nowhere and barely had a signal, but 911 is supposed to connect no matter what.

It wouldn't.

He was running behind me.

I tried again, crying out, "God, please!"

My hands shaking.

My uninjured eye barely focusing.

This time it rang.

"911, what is your emergency?"

"I need an ambulance, immediately. My boyfriend beat me up. I'm in so much pain."

They started asking me questions. What happened? Where was I? Where was he?

Where was he?

He had walked to our truck. He kept a gun in that truck. I could barely see anything. I ran to the front of our deck. He had something in his hand, but I couldn't see.

I responded, "He's here."

Damon yelled, "Tell them I'll be waiting down the hill for them."

Before help arrived, Damon's mom showed up. She looked at me shocked and horrified and shook her face. "What did you do to make him do this?"

I was on the phone for twenty-five minutes before the police arrived. One township car. One sheriff.

We knew the township cop; he took one look at me, and I could see the shock on his face.

As we walked into the house, Damon's mom stood there with his two oldest children. My heart ached that they had to see me like that.

The police immediately split us up.

They had him sit at the kitchen table, while I went into the bathroom.

The township cop was with him. The sheriff was with me.

I told the sheriff I couldn't see and explained my glasses had fallen when he attacked me. The sheriff asked Damon to go grab my glasses.

They allowed him to bring them to me. When he handed them to me, he said "Great. Now we're both going to jail tonight."

When he left, I looked at the sheriff and asked, "Am I going to go to jail tonight?" He looked at me and quietly said "No. You're going to the hospital."

He asked if there was anyone I could call, since my kids were in bed asleep.

I tried to call my mom, but she didn't answer. I called my nineteen-year-old son who lived with them, thankfully he answered. It was almost four o'clock in the morning. I told him what happened and he couldn't believe it. He woke up my mom, and she was there within ten minutes.

When she walked in and saw me, she turned around and looked at him sitting at the table and said "You piece of shit. You call yourself a man. Look what you did to her?!."

Damon calmly replied, "It was self-defense."

The ambulance finally arrived forty-five minutes later.

I was in immense pain. If you've ever had a broken bone, then you know the burning sensation that comes with it.

The entire left side of my face burned fiercely. My body was aching everywhere.

They helped me walk down the hill and into the ambulance.

When I stepped into the ambulance, the first responders couldn't hide their reaction - horror.

They took my vitals. My heartbeat was elevated; my blood pressure was through the roof. The ride to the hospital was long and bumpy. Pain came with every bump in the road.

When I arrived at the hospital, my mom was there.

She managed to wake the kids and get them into her car in time for them to watch Damon be handcuffed and loaded into the sheriff's car. His kids had already been taken by his mother.

They began to photograph me like a crime scene. Because I was one.

They had a special camera and ruler, and the nurses very carefully began to assess me starting at my feet.

I had several cuts on my toes and feet; the camera shuttered.

Next, my upper left thigh and buttocks. The bruising was already forming.

My arms were next; they too had cuts and showed bruising going up to my shoulder.

My neck was beginning to bruise in the shape of a hand.

Then there was my face.

My left eye swollen shut, purple. When they opened it to shine a flashlight, it was bloody on the inside. Broken blood vessels.

There was swelling and bruising on my cheekbone.

The bottom of my jaw began to swell.

My mom sat by my bedside as I was examined.

The doctor came in and moved my throat gently to ensure nothing had been damaged.

They gave me some medicine for the pain and ordered x-rays.

While I was returning from my x-ray, the side effects of the pain medication began.

My body does not handle medication well, particularly pain medicine. I was about to vomit. I asked the transporter to stop. I didn't want my mom to witness this. I was about to vomit with a broken, dislocated jaw. She had seen enough already.

The doctor told me I had a multi-point orbital fracture, two breaks in the bones surrounding my left eye socket. He explained that the orbital rim is one of the hardest structures in the face to break. I hadn't just bruised my cheek or cracked a bone, I had fractured the very

structure that protects my eye, my
vision, my brain, my life.

He said blunt-force trauma that severe
can cause permanent damage to
eyesight, crush nerves, or radiate enough
force to fracture the skull. Hearing that, I
understood the truth: I had walked out
of that night alive by a miracle.

Their imaging machine wasn't detailed
enough to fully evaluate facial fractures,
so they referred me to an oral and
maxillofacial surgeon.

When I met with him a couple of days
later, he delivered the next round of
news: my jaw had been both dislocated
and fractured.

They gave me some pain medicine and
sent me home with my mom.

The next morning, my kids wanted to
come see me.

I prepared myself the best I could before
they came in.

My mom brought my four youngest
children into her bedroom where I lay.

The shock on their faces, I'll never forget.

They left the room and shortly after my phone rang. It was the police department; they needed to come and take my statement. During our conversation I remembered that I had never stopped my voice recording. I had recorded the entire event on audio! I let them know, and they said they would need that if I could send it to them. I told them that wouldn't be an issue.

I hung up with them and an hour later a number from out of state that I didn't recognize was calling me.

I answered it.

"Hey. How are you doing?"

My heart fell into the pit of my stomach.

It was Damon.

Reflection

If you have ever been on the receiving end of violence, whether physical, emotional, or verbal, I want you to hear this clearly: nothing you did caused it, invited it, or made it okay. Responsibility belongs to the person who chose to harm.

If you have never experienced this and you find yourself trying to understand how something like this happens, I want to say this gently: it can feel easier to question the victim than to hold the abuser fully accountable. But the truth is simple. Abuse is a choice.

Sometimes we live through things that shock us to our core. If this chapter brought anything up for you, you do not have to figure it all out right now. You only have to take the next right breath, and then the next.

A Note to You

Whatever you're feeling right now is okay. If this touched your own story, someone you love, or something you never expected to read, you're not wrong for how it's landing. Take this at your pace.

Rebel Rising

You don't have to write anything here. Just remember what happened to you, or what happened to someone you love, was not your fault. That truth clears the way for you to rise without carrying what was never yours.

Chapter 22

Aftermath

My mind was spinning. Hearing his voice sent chills down my spine. Why was he calling me? I was still reeling. My jaw was so swollen, and my face burned where it had been broken. I could barely speak.

I think I said something like, "You broke my orbital and my jaw."

He replied, "What are you talking about?"

I hung up.

I blocked the number.

Not long after, the police arrived to take my statement. My parents sat with me while I had to recount the night before, every detail, every piece of it.

They took their own photos, too. The bruising on my neck had started to bloom, and you could see the remnants of a perfect handprint.

My back was bruised and marked,
including bite marks from when we were
intimate. I hadn't fully understood it
until then, but it was another form of
physical abuse. He would bite me so
hard that my skin would bleed.

My left thigh and buttock were badly
bruised from where he had thrown me
against the wall with the mattress.

After the police left, my mom and I
started planning how to get me out, and
fast. I was sure he would be released on
Monday. It was the weekend, so he
couldn't appear in front of a judge yet.

I gathered a group of friends, my mom,
and my kids, and we went back to the
house to pack up everything we could.

My friends and my mom insisted I take
all of our food, but I couldn't bring
myself to leave his children without it. It
wasn't just about him.

I wasn't much help those two days. The
pain was unbearable. I can't take pain
medication other than Tylenol, and it
barely touched it.

Here's a clean rewrite that keeps your voice, keeps the facts, and tightens the courtroom sequence. I also filled in the grand jury's indictment explanation in a way that's accurate and readable, without getting overly legal.

Monday morning came and I got a call. I would have to attend his bond hearing that Wednesday. They told me I would have a court advocate there to support me.

I had never been through anything in court before. I had no idea what to expect. My nerves were shot. I met my court advocate, but if I'm being honest, she wasn't much of a comfort. She sat off to the side on her phone and didn't offer much guidance or reassurance.

They told me Damon would be attending virtually. He was at the county jail about thirty minutes away, and this was during Covid. They also told me the officers who had responded that night would testify, and so would I.

The prosecution and his defense attorney would both ask questions. This hearing was to determine what his bond would be.

The prosecutor told me they were charging him with an F2 felony, the second most serious level. They couldn't charge him for attempted murder, even though that's what it felt like.

They called me up first. I was relieved that I couldn't see him on the screen. The idea of looking at him again made my stomach turn.

The judge started the hearing and asked Damon if he could hear it. Damon acted like he couldn't. I'm almost certain it was an act. He knew if he claimed he couldn't "hear," they would bring him out of his cell and into the courthouse.

And that's exactly what happened.

About an hour later, I saw them walking him down the hall in an orange jumpsuit, shackled at the hands and feet. I felt like I was going to vomit.

My body was still in shock, and the pain was everywhere, especially in my face and jaw. I could barely speak through the swelling, dislocation, and damage.

Then they called my name.

How was I supposed to look at him?

The bailiff leaned toward me and said, "It's okay. Just look to the right. You don't have to look at him."

My left eye was still swollen shut, so that helped a little.

I sat down and they swore me in.

The prosecuting attorney asked general questions about the night of the assault. Then it was his attorney's turn. I knew him. I don't know if he remembered me, but I remembered him from something I dealt with back in my teens.

Every answer sent pain shooting through my face and mouth. Talking felt impossible.

Then his attorney asked how many children I had.

"Five," I said.

He asked if all five were there that night.

"Four of them," I replied.

He asked what they were doing at the time.

"Sleeping."

Then he asked, "Do they all have the same father?"

I waited for the prosecutor to object. She didn't.

I said, "I don't see how that is relevant."

The entire courtroom gasped.

His attorney snapped back, "That's up for the judge to decide."

Thankfully, the judge stepped in and agreed with me. That was the end of his questioning.

I was dismissed and went back to wait while the officers testified. When they were finished, we waited again.

Then came the best news.

His bond was set at half a million dollars.

If he wanted out, he would have to post ten percent or sit in jail until trial.

Not knowing whether his family would pay it, I applied for a temporary restraining order. I also had to petition to get the only key to the truck. He had taken his keys with him, thinking it would keep me from accessing it. But I had the title showing joint ownership, and I was able to retrieve the key.

His family chose not to pay his bond.

He was charged with a second-degree felony and entered a plea of not guilty.

The case was then sent to a grand jury, where the prosecution had to determine whether there was enough evidence to formally indict him and move the case forward.

I had never even heard of that before. No one prepares you for how much of this is a process.

A grand jury indictment is when the prosecutor presents the basics of the case to a group of citizens called a grand jury.

The grand jury's job is not to decide guilt or innocence. Their job is to decide whether there is enough evidence to formally move the case forward on felony charges. If they believe there is, they issue an indictment, which is the official charging document that takes the case into the next stage.

I was standing at the beginning of that road, realizing it was going to be longer than I ever imagined.

I applied for a leave of absence from my job and worked with HR to turn in everything they needed. I had constant doctor appointments while I healed, and because of my jaw, I was put on a mostly liquid diet. Baby food. Yogurt. Anything I could swallow without pain.

After six weeks off, I was expected to return to work. I didn't feel ready, but I didn't have a choice. I still had to provide for my children.

I also didn't know where we were going to live. We were still staying with my parents. I still had the house I was purchasing on a land contract, but I knew one day Damon would get out, and I didn't feel safe there anymore, not with him living so close to my parents.

I started thinking about moving back to Myrtle Beach. Dave, my ex-husband and my daughter's dad, had already moved to Florida, so it didn't matter if I stayed in Ohio or not.

Surprisingly, Doyle and another friend offered to help clean out and remodel the house so the kids and I could live there. And because it looked like the court process was going to take a while, I decided to stay for the time being.

Then the triggers started showing up in ways I didn't understand.

One night my parents were watching TV and they were recapping a boxing match. The sound of punches landing hit me like a flashback. My heart started racing. The room felt like it was spinning. I couldn't stay there. I had to get outside for air, fast.

The following week I had to return to work, virtually. I was getting ready for a sales call on Zoom, and about ten minutes before the call, my body started shaking. I couldn't breathe. My heart was pounding so hard I thought something was seriously wrong.

What was happening to me?

I told my mom about the panic, nightmares, and foggy thoughts. How jumpy I had become. How aware I was of every sound, every shift, every doorway.

She looked at me and said, "Janice, I think you might have PTSD."

PTSD. I remember thinking, "No. That's for veterans. Not me."

But I started researching it anyway.

She was right.

I had every symptom.

I searched for a therapist and made a call for the earliest appointment I could get.

I'll never forget sitting in the waiting room for that first visit. I was shaking like a leaf. The scratch on my left cheek was still visible. I could see out of my left eye again, but it was still bloodshot inside. My jaw was still swollen. Bruises still covered my body.

Then I heard a soft voice say my name.

"Janice."

I looked up to see a short, middle-aged woman with shoulder-length brown hair and glasses. She smiled gently and motioned for me to follow her.

I sat down in a black leather chair. I had withered down to nearly nothing from the liquid diet. That chair felt like it could swallow me whole.

And then it began.

She asked me to tell her what happened.

After a few visits, she gave me a formal diagnosis.

I did have PTSD.

Being diagnosed with PTSD wasn't about one traumatic event. It was about years of unprocessed experiences, starting in childhood, compounded by hard encounters along the way. The final event didn't create the trauma; it revealed how much I had been carrying for so long.

She tried EMDR, tapping, and grounding. For some people it helps, but for me it didn't feel soothing. It felt triggering. I wasn't an easy case.

And after that panic attack before the sales call, one thing became painfully clear.

I could not do my job the way I used to.

Being on a phone or zoom call had become one of my biggest triggers. Maybe because of those twenty-five minutes on the phone with 911, fighting for my life, waiting for help to arrive. I don't know. I just knew I couldn't force my body past it.

I applied for short-term disability and kept going to therapy, hoping it would get me back to where I had been.

I went weekly.

Work demanded that I return.

I wasn't ready.

I asked for accommodations. I worked with my therapist to outline them clearly and submitted everything to HR.

HR came back and asked how long I would have my condition.

My condition.

PTSD.

How long would I have PTSD for?

My therapist couldn't believe what they were asking. They wanted an end date. An expiration date for trauma.

That isn't how it works.

She responded in detail. The accommodation was necessary. The timeline was uncertain. It depended on my recovery.

I had been nearly strangled and beaten to death, and now this major corporation, the owner of the largest newspaper and print magazine in the United States, wanted a timeline for how long I would be affected by it.

When HR and my manager didn't get the answer they wanted, the next shoe dropped.

They terminated me.

Reflection

Keep Going

There are seasons when life hits hard, and the world still expects you to function. You still get the kids to school, show up to work, answer the phone, pay the bills, and keep moving, even when something inside you is still trying to catch up. That isn't "fine." That's resilience.

A Note to You

If you're getting through a season on sheer will, you're not failing because it feels hard. You're carrying a lot. Give yourself credit for what you're doing, even if no one else can see the weight.

Rebel Rising

Finish this sentence:
Even when I don't feel strong, I can still

Chapter 23

Limbo

A couple of months passed by, and it was time for the Grand Jury appearance. I was really nervous, but I didn't know what to expect. This time I had to go by myself.

I was greeted by the prosecuting attorney. A nice older gentleman, very tall, big wired framed glasses, an older pinstripe gray suit, and a gentle smile. He instructed me as to what I could expect. He comforted me in knowing that I would not have to encounter Damon's attorney that day. No interrogation for me.

He said that the county's prosecuting attorney would be asking me questions as to what happened the night of my assault and that all I had to do was walk them through what happened and answer the questions.

To him, it sounded simple. To me, it felt unbearable.

I was being asked to relive it again.

The swelling in my eye had gone down some, but the scratch on my cheek was still visible. My jaw still ached, and every time I spoke, the pain flared. It seemed to hurt more each time I told the story, as if my body remembered before my mind could catch up.

A month earlier, I had already been forced to retell everything during the hearing for my restraining order. That one had been over the phone because of Covid, but it didn't matter. Each time I told it, I was right back there. Every sound. Every movement. Every moment.

When it was time, I sat before the Grand Jury and answered the prosecutor's questions. I focused on staying present. On breathing. On getting through it.

Afterward, the jury was given an opportunity to ask questions.

There was a pause.

Then a woman, around sixty years old with short blonde hair, spoke up.

"Has he ever done anything like this before?"

I hated that question.

Not because of the answer, but because of what it implied.

Questions like that quietly shift responsibility. They suggest that violence only counts if it happens more than once. That context somehow excuses and condones brutality.

I answered quietly, "No."

That was my truth at the time.

I hadn't yet fully recognized the warning signs for what they were. Looking back, there were many things. But none of that made what happened to me acceptable.

After my testimony, the police chief was brought in to answer their questions. I was asked to wait.

Minutes passed.
Then more.

Time stretched until it felt suspended.

I sat there, stuck in limbo, waiting to find out whether my life would move forward or stall yet again.

Finally, my phone rang.

The prosecutor told me that the Grand Jury had found enough evidence to move forward.

There would be an arraignment scheduled for a later date.

Step one was complete.

Step two was coming.

As I tried to mentally prepare for what lay ahead, I found myself focused on something else. The scars on my back.

I knew I couldn't want to erase them, but I didn't want them to be the first thing I saw when I looked at myself either.

I started searching for tattoo ideas and came across an image of a woman with angel wings spread across her back. The moment I saw it, I knew. Wings made sense. They symbolized rebirth. Survival. Faith. Protection. But it still felt unfinished.

I decided to pair them with a quote that would run down my spine in delicate script:

"She dipped her wings in ink to cover up her scars."

The process took nearly sixteen hours, spread across several days. It was painful, exhausting, and strangely grounding.

There was something deeply poignant about enduring that pain by choice, about sitting with it, breathing through it, and transforming it into something intentional.

It felt like I was reclaiming those scarred places.

Not hiding them, not denying them, but rewriting the story they told.

Now, when I look at my back, I don't just see what was done to me.

I see what I survived.

I see faith.

I see strength.

I see wings.

And I carry them with me.

In fact, you may have even noticed them on the cover of this book.

Reflection

In Between

We have all encountered limbo or an in between season. It is exhausting because it keeps you waiting while your life is still moving. You can be doing everything right and still feel suspended. That space does not mean nothing is happening.

A Note to You

If you are going through a season of limbo, hang in there. I know it is so difficult at times. It tries our patience and strength. Eventually, you will come out of it.

Rebel Rising

What's one thing you can do for yourself
while you wait that helps you feel a little
steadier?

Chapter 24

The Plea

Then arraignment day came.

The prosecutor had emailed me that Damon was planning on pleading guilty.

Arraignment day arrived, and with it, a weight I didn't know how to name.

This was the point where Damon would formally enter his plea.

Not guilty.

Hearing those words I halfheartedly had been expecting, even though hearing it still felt surreal. When I heard from the prosecutor, he was planning on pleading guilty; I didn't believe it.

Now here he was pleading not guilty. As if denying what he had done could somehow undo the damage to my body, my mind, my life.

Then the moment that shocked us all.

His defense attorney requested the judge to allow him to recuse himself. His client was refusing to work with him. He was also refusing to take the plea deal he felt was favorable and in his best interest.

The judge filled Damon in as to what would happen if his attorney would recuse himself.

Damon's Dad was livid. They asked us to leave the courtroom so that Damon, his attorney, and his father could all speak.

His father did not think he should plead guilty.

The man that I once looked up to and loved like a father had turned against me. He sided with Damon. He believed his story that I simply "fell out of bed." He felt that Damon could get off scot-free.

If Damon were to choose to have another attorney, it would be months or up to a year before it would go to trial. Which meant sitting in jail waiting. Logistically, it didn't make sense for Damon.

Take the plea, do the same amount of time as waiting on a new attorney and trial.

Take the trial, do eight to twelve years.

The prosecutor had explained to me beforehand what his pleading guilty would get him.

If Damon pled guilty, the state would recommend two to three years in prison. No probation. No early release built into the agreement. But there was a condition.

I had to agree.

I was given time to think.

What no one tells you about moments like this is how heavy choice feels when you are already depleted. This wasn't about mercy. It wasn't about forgiveness. It was about survival.

I didn't want to spend years reliving the worst night of my life in a courtroom. I didn't want my children dragged through it. I didn't want to sit across from him again and again, waiting for verdicts and delays and appeals.

I wanted it to stop.

So, I agreed.

After Damon was done speaking with his father and attorney, he changed his mind.

Damon pleaded guilty.

Upon his pleading guilty, his father made a request to receive all of the guns that had been confiscated after my assault. As a felon, Damon is no longer allowed to own a firearm.

The judge granted his request. Releasing all of the guns to his father. He claimed he was going to sell them to help pay his attorney fees. I'm not so confident about that.

I was given the opportunity to read my victim impact statement. Standing there, I said what I needed to say. Not for him, but for me.

Here is my statement exactly as I gave it that day.

It's difficult to put into words all of the physical, mental, emotional pain and trauma that has been caused, not only to me, but my family and my children, that have had to witness my journey since my assault four months ago.

The actions of Damon Rottenburger have changed my life forever. I can't begin to describe the terror I felt the very early morning I was assaulted. I truly thought I was going to die, that he was going to kill me, and still fear for my life once he is done serving his sentence.

I often think of how he must regret letting me go. I constantly relive my attack through flashbacks and nightmares on a daily basis, due to the PTSD I now suffer from. Even writing this is causing me to have a panic attack. My heart begins to race, my breathing ceases, and the room starts to darken. Re-telling my story, my nightmare, takes a lot out of me, but I know how important it is that you, your honor, hear it.

Sleeping is nearly impossible for me these days because of the defendant waking me right before he attacked me. He told me to get out of the bed and when I refused he picked it up until I rolled out, having nowhere to go, but landing on top of the stand and contractor bags of shoes I had beside me, there was no open floor access; once I was out he continued to push the mattress against me, causing me to hit the wall and bruise my leg. I pushed back until the bed landed back down, albeit not level. When I stood on the bed and confronted him for doing this, he grabbed me by my throat, we slid down the bed and he began strangling me, while sitting on top of me. I was naked and blind, as I could hardly see at all without my contacts or glasses. I fought while he strangled me and eventually got him to stop by putting my thumbs in his eyes. I told him we were done, he spit on me, I called him a name, and he punched me 3 or 4 times, that I can recall.

I remember the first punch, it was to my left eye, it immediately swelled and I felt horrific burning. I remember him punching my face a couple more times, and the moment my jaw broke, I felt it shift and tasted the blood. When he was done, I somehow managed to get out from under him and I tried to find my phone. I had a hard time since I couldn't see and he was quickly behind me. I found my phone on the floor under the bed and he snatched it from me. I told him he broke my jaw and I needed 911. He refused to give me my phone. I ran to the bathroom to look at my face, covering myself with a towel. I looked in the mirror and my eye was swollen shut, my face was bruised, swollen, and bleeding from where his thumbnail had left a deep scratch, my entire face burned and throbbed horribly.

Damon came into the bathroom, took one look at me and said I shouldn't have done that. I'm going to jail for Father's day Janice, aren't I, and I said yes you are, give me my phone, which he still refused. I ran to our bedroom door, cracked it open and yelled for my 13 year old son to call 911, he slammed the door shut. I elbowed Damon, grabbed my phone and ran outside on our balcony to call 911 since I had no signal in the house. I kept trying to get a signal for my call to go through, begging God and Jesus to please have my call go through so someone could help me. I thought a signal wasn't needed for

*a 911 call to complete but it wasn't working
and I was extremely terrified he was going to
hurt me more or kill me. He was outside with
me now, behind me, following me around,
begging me not to call. I thought he may just
decide to throw me off of our 2 story balcony
or go grab one of the guns and shoot me. I just
kept telling him to stay away from me.*

*I was frightened my children may wake up
and hear the commotion, because my boys
room was right next to where we were. I was
in indescribable pain. By the grace of God my
call finally connected. It took the police and
ambulance 25 minutes to arrive. 25 minutes
that I was terrified that at any given moment
he would kill me.*

*Once the police arrived on scene, the officer
immediately took one look at my face and
called for an ambulance. We went into the
house and they separated us, I went in the
bathroom, he went in the kitchen. I couldn't
see and the officer asked me where my glasses
were, I was unsure so they allowed Damon to
go find them for me. When he brought them to*

me he made it a point to tell me I was going to go to jail too. He wasn't done scaring me.

The ambulance arrived, the officer walked me down, I could barely see so my mom had to assist him. They took my blood pressure, it was insanely high, 180 over 105. This was nearly an hour after the assault took place. They had nothing to give me for the pain. I had to wait 25 minutes for us to get to the hospital and into the ER. The entire time the pain was absolutely horrendous. They finally gave me something for pain at the hospital, but even then it didn't help much. I had a lot of blood running to my stomach from all the breaks, which caused horrible vomiting. Imagine trying to vomit with a broken jaw. It was the worst thing ever. I was so thankful my mother was in the waiting room, and I was in the hall where she couldn't witness it. It was hard enough on her to have to see me this way.

I was discharged a few hours later and went to my parents house. My mom had taken my four minor children there. I will never forget the look on their faces when they saw me, and I know they will never forget seeing their mom that way. My 13 year old son felt horrible guilt for not waking up and helping me. I tell him all the time how thankful I am he didn't wake up. I don't know what Damon would have done, especially if he would have tried stopping him.

I suffered two breaks in my left orbital, a busted blood vessel in my eye, a fractured jaw on my left side, a contusion to my right jaw from the impact my left side took, a small scar (which thankfully makeup covers up) on my cheek from the cut his thumbnail left. You may notice that I have some difficulty speaking. This may be permanent. I still do not have full use of my jaw, it is still healing. For the first 2 months after my assault my children couldn't just run at me and hug me, they had to tell me they wanted a hug, because one little bump and I would have needed surgery. I still have to be careful, my Dad went to hug me the other day and a little push against my jaw when he squeezed me was excruciating. I couldn't eat anything but baby food for two months and still struggle to eat solid food, especially on my broken side. My eye is still not healed. It is still sore and swollen. I have permanent nerve damage and sometimes lose my vision or have blurry vision in my eye. The back of my head had a tire like swelling from hitting it off the wood floor when he punched me. I had bruises on my neck from him strangling me, and on my left thigh when he had pushed the bed against me. I had bruises on my back from hitting the floor. I see a therapist twice a week for my PTSD, and am working through my triggers. The first 2 months I had to take FMLA from work because of my injuries, losing some income I needed as a single mother and being left with hospital and doctor bills from what my insurance didn't cover. I recently went back on FMLA because of the issues I am having with my PTSD and the increase of stress from the upcoming court hearing.

My only daughter, who is 5, tells me all the time that she is afraid Damon will kill me when he gets out. She feels safer that he is in jail and that she won't be losing her only mommy. She has nightmares several times a week about him hurting or killing me and fears growing up and having this happen to her. She will begin seeing a therapist soon.

I am pleading with the court to take Damon Rottenburger's actions seriously. He didn't just assault me, he tried to kill me, and I fully believe he will try again when he is released. He has already tried to contact me since being in jail, has requested a mutual friend to talk me into changing my story, has given a note to his parents asking for me to return a gun to him that I do not possess and if I did I would have given it to the police, not the defendant. While he may be banned from owning or possessing a firearm, he is well versed in how to build one untraceable. We had around 35 taken from the home that were his, and he still has others that were not taken into possession by the police that he gave to friends and his children's mother. His father has voiced his intention on buying them all back, and I do not feel safe in this knowledge, since his father is known for catering to him, even when he knows he's in the wrong. The defendant has not shown an ounce of remorse or sympathy in his actions. He has had conversations with others since my assault where he blames me and calls me horrible names.

Your honor, I know that the recommendation is that the defendant receive a minimum of two years in prison to a maximum of three, however, I do not feel that is long enough for the person who tried to kill me. While the court system may look at him as someone without a criminal history, I implore you to look at his actions, the severity of my injuries, along with the knowledge he has with weapons, and give him a longer sentence.

A few people have said that they bet I can't wait for this court hearing to be over so I could put this all behind me, but the truth is, this will never be behind me. It is forever a part of me, it changed me and my life forever, it is a battle I have to go through and live through every day. Knowing he will one day walk free again. The assault won't be behind me, but this part of it will be.

After I read my statement. I sat down. Quiet tears streamed down my cheeks.

My attorney and Mom sat with me, each squeezing a hand.

The judge thanked me for being so brave in giving my statement that day. Everything after that sounded like Charlie Brown's Mom. Muddled words.

What I did make out was his sentence.

Two years. No chance of probation.

I thought the chapter was finally closing that day, but I was wrong.

After his plea, life tested me again.

My daughter, strong-willed and independent like her mother, had just taught herself how to ride her bike. She rode over to the neighbor's driveway because they had concrete and we had gravel. As she tried to turn, she lost control and fell, landing directly on her head.

Our neighbor, nearly deaf, heard her crying and brought her home.

I knew immediately something was wrong.

She began showing signs of a concussion, and being twenty-five minutes from the nearest hospital, I didn't wait. I ran her to the car and started driving. About a mile down the road, she began to vomit.

I pulled into the emergency room and ran inside carrying her, yelling "head injury." It felt like a scene from a television show. They rushed her back immediately.

The first doctor told me she was fine.

The second, a young resident, insisted on a CT scan.

That scan changed everything.

She had two skull fractures and a small brain bleed.

Within minutes, we were being prepped for transport. The next thing I knew, we were in a helicopter, lifting off and heading to Children's Hospital in Pittsburgh. We landed on the roof and rushed inside.

We stayed there for four days.

She was okay.
She is okay.

She still struggles with some memory issues, but she survived.

And so, did I.

Another emergency.
Another decision was made under pressure.
Another reminder that even in the aftermath, life kept asking more of me.

Reflection

Carrying the Weight

There are moments when you are asked to make decisions you never wanted to make. Not because they feel right, but because you need the chaos to stop. Choice, in those moments, doesn't feel empowered. Sometimes we don't get relief. We just go forward.

A Note to You

If you've ever had to decide while already exhausted, hurting, or scared, give yourself grace. Survival choices are still choices, even when they don't feel like victories.

Rebel Rising

What is one decision you made because you needed things to stop, not because it was easy or fair?

Chapter 25

Here We Go Again

A year had gone by when I received an unexpected letter from the county court. Damon had requested a judicial release.

A judicial release is a request made by an incarcerated person asking a judge to reduce their prison sentence and release them early under supervision.

It is not an appeal.
It does not overturn a conviction.
It is essentially asking the judge for leniency after sentencing.

After serving out a required portion of his sentence, Damon was legally allowed to file this motion. It went back to the same court and the same judge who had sentenced him. The judge could consider factors like his behavior while incarcerated, participation in programs, and whether they believed he could be safely released back into the community.

The judge can consider several factors, including behavior while incarcerated, participation in programs, and whether they believe the person can be safely released into the community.

The victim is notified.
The victim has the right to be present.
The victim has the right to speak.

If a judicial release is denied, it is typically final for that stage of the sentence. In most cases, the person is not supposed to be able to request it again unless circumstances significantly change, or the law allows for another filing window.

In my case, his first request was denied.

Which was expected and a huge relief. I believed it meant the sentence would finally stand.

I was wrong.

Sixty days later, Damon requested another judicial release.

This time the judge was open to having a hearing.

Once again, we were back in the courtroom. Again, we went over to his guilty plea and what it meant. Once again, I had to explain how damaging it was for me to be there, reliving everything I had worked so hard to survive.

This time, they allowed the mother of his children to come into the courtroom to read a statement on his behalf. She spoke about him as a father. About his character. About why he deserved another chance.

She did not mention the years of abuse she herself had endured.

I understood why.
She is still tied to him.
I am not.

Once again, I was given the opportunity to read a Victim Impact Statement. A new one. One that carried the weight of everything that had happened since the last time I stood in that room.

Your Honor,

Just a little over a year ago we were all in this courtroom awaiting to hear which way Damon would go with his plea. He was to plead guilty, changed his mind to not guilty, then changed it again, back to guilty. I read my first VIS at that time where I told my story of how he attacked, strangled, and beat me; causing two breaks to my eye along with my jaw. As you can probably assume, I am not happy to hear that he is trying to get out early, or that the court is willing to listen to his plea. I won't assume that you remember me or my story, as I know you've heard many over the past year. I also choose not to re-tell it in this VIS due to my PTSD from this assault.

A year ago, the defendant pled guilty over taking his chances of going in front of a jury that if found guilty, would have given him a much longer sentence. When he pled guilty, you asked him several pointed questions, making sure he understood his decision. Every one of those questions asked he answered yes to. The only thing concerning him was losing his guns and gun rights as a felon. So, I'm a bit confused as to why Damon thinks he can now go back on his agreement to the minimum of two years that he accepted when he pled guilty, which was done out of cowardice, and not out of remorse or accountability. Remorse that he has still not shown, and guilt that he still is unable to take full accountability for.

His institutional report you have received today will probably say he's been a great inmate and done some courses and anger management etc, etc. He's a great manipulator, I know. He learned from one of the best, and he sits in support of his son. My children have had to deal with the bullying due to these events because they attend school with his nephew that lives with his parents and he has repeatedly told them I got what I deserved and his uncle shouldn't be in prison for it. I'm sure he didn't come up with that sentiment on his own.

My parents are neighbors to the Rottenburg family. Damon and I resided in the neighboring home to his parents and to my knowledge, he plans to return to it once released. This is not comfortable for me or my family as there is only one road leading to and from the neighborhood in which they all live, meaning our chance of crossing paths is good. I kindly request that he is not allowed to live within 3 miles of my parents, as my children and I frequent there daily. I have a civil protection order on him for myself, and while that provides some peace of mind in some instances, it doesn't in others. I also request that my parents be granted an order of civil protection from him, which I believe they should have due to Damon's past of flying drones over their property and along with the uncertainty that his father obtained the

guns that were taken from our home that he owned, as I understand it was his father's intention on obtaining. While I know it isn't legal for him to own or possess, that doesn't mean it will stop him as he believes he is above the law, and his move for an early judicial release today shows just that. I have faith, your honor, that you will make the best decision for everyone and will do what you feel will keep me, my children, and my family

*safe from the person who tried to end my life
on June 21, 2020, but did not succeed.*

Respectfully,

Janice Becker

The last time I had read my statement to the court, I had done so by looking down and making sure that I, in no way, made eye contact with Damon. That was not the case on this day.

On this day, I looked right at him when I spoke.

My voice didn't tremble like it did the last time.

Tears didn't stream down my face.

My body wasn't healing like last time, but something else had changed.

I stood as a survivor.

A warrior.

To my surprise, when I was done and sat down, Damon spun

around from his seat and said, "Janice, I sincerely apologize for that. I wish it never happened."

I knew that apology was for what he did to me. It was that it landed him in a seat of accountability, and one he wanted out of.

The judge instructed him to stop
speaking to me. Then, to my disbelief,
she thanked him for his apology and said
she appreciated it.

She proceeded to say she was granting
his judicial release.

The anger rose up into my throat.
The sound in the room faded away.
Once again, the judge's voice turned
into Charlie Brown's teacher, muffled
and distant.

When my hearing returned, she was
addressing me.

She explained that had Damon served
the original two-year sentence; he would
not have been placed on probation. With
this release, he would be. He would be
sent to a transitional center, allowed to
leave during the day to work, but
required to return each night.

He would continue anger management.

She listed approximately sixteen stipulations tied to his release.

The most important ones were these:
He could not have any contact with me or my family.
He had to maintain full-time employment.
He could not leave the state without permission.
He was ordered to pay restitution for the medical expenses I incurred due to my injuries.

His probation officer was assigned right there in the courtroom.

The officer took my number and assured me we would be in frequent contact so I would feel safe.

When we left the courtroom and walked toward the parking lot, his parents and the mother of his children were outside. They were celebrating. Laughing. Calling me names.

It took everything in me not to react to the way I wanted that day.

Three months later, Damon was released.

Shortly after that he ran into my mom at the gas station down from their house. He said hello to her, in a cocky way of course. Of course. My Mom shot back, "Don't speak to me."

"Bitch!" he yelled. "I'll say whatever I want."I immediately called his probation officer to report it and was told that I needed proof.

When we reached out to the gas station for their video footage, it had conveniently been deleted.

Damon did just what I said he would.

He drove past my house frequently.

Flew a drone over it, like I had predicted.

I never received a single dollar of restitution.

He did not maintain full-time employment. Instead, he claimed he was working for his father.

It became painfully clear that he had walked away without the accountability the judge had intended.

It also became clear that I could not stay.

Being there, in that town, was suffocating. I had outgrown it.

Then I saw a post on LinkedIn from a professional connection. They were looking for a Media Director.

It was perfect.

I applied.
I got the job.
And two months later, I moved.

Reflection

Knowing When It's Time

There comes a point when you realize the situation isn't going to change enough to keep you safe, whole, or at peace. You've spoken up. You've waited. You've hoped the right people would do the right thing. And then it becomes clear: staying is costing you more than leaving ever could.

A Note to You

If you've reached a place where you know you can't stay anymore, trust that knowing. It doesn't make you dramatic or impatient. It means you're listening to yourself. As you should.

Rebel Rising

Where did you finally realize it was time to go, and what helped you choose yourself when you did?

Chapter 26

A Fresh Start

Moving is never easy, but I'd like to think I became something of an expert at it.

If you've been keeping count, this was our ninth move in just six years.

Each move carried its own weight. Boxes weren't just filled with clothes and furniture; they were filled with memories, decisions, and survival. I had learned how to pack quickly, how to detach just enough to keep going, how to make anywhere feel temporary because permanence had never felt safe.

This time was different.

At first, I worried I wouldn't find a home large enough for all of us. I worried about affordability, about schools, and about whether I was making the right decision yet again. But once more, God came through in a way that felt undeniable.

We found a beautiful five-bedroom home with three and a half bathrooms, a three-car garage, and a large front and backyard. It sat in a quiet neighborhood that looked like it belonged on the Hallmark Channel. The kind of place where kids rode bikes, neighbors waved, and the air felt calmer the moment you pulled in.

The schools were highly rated, and more importantly, they were kind. When I explained that we were relocating under difficult circumstances, they didn't ask invasive questions. They asked how they could help.

That alone felt like a miracle.

The move itself was exhausting. My body was still healing. My nervous system was still on edge. But there was something steady underneath it all, a sense that this time, we were not running. We were choosing.

I'll never forget our first night in the new house.

After unpacking what we could and getting the kids settled, I tucked my daughter into bed. She curled up under her blanket like she had always belonged there. When I turned off the light and stepped back into the hallway, I felt something loosen inside me.

I sat down at the top of the stairs.

Silent tears streamed down my face, but they weren't tears of grief or fear. They were tears of gratitude. Of disbelief. Of relief.

I whispered thank you to God over and over. Thank you for getting us here. Thank you for protecting us. Thank you for not letting the worst moments of my life be the final ones.

For the first time in a very long time, my body wasn't bracing for what might happen next.

We were safe.

We were home.

In the weeks that followed, I noticed small things beginning to change. The kids slept better. I slept better. I no longer jumped at every sound. I could sit in the quiet without my thoughts racing.

I started to imagine a future again, not just survival plans.

This house wasn't just a place to live. It was proof. Proof that the story didn't end where it almost did. Proof that rebuilding was possible. Proof that God had not abandoned me in the darkest chapters, even when I had felt completely alone.

I didn't know then what challenges still lay ahead. I didn't know how much strength I would still be asked to find.

But I knew this:

We had crossed something invisible but permanent.

This wasn't an escape.

This was a fresh start.

Reflection

New Chapter

Freedom can be quiet, but it is still freedom. There are moments when you look around and realize you built your way out. You made the call. You did the work. You got yourself to a new place, whether that was a job or home, and you did not need anyone's permission to choose better. If you've ever started over and felt proud of yourself, hold onto that. That's the Rebel in you.

A Note to You

If you're in a season where you're starting or building something new, I'm proud of you. You deserve to feel excited about what is ahead.

Rebel Rising

Where in your life are you ready for a fresh start, and what is the first step you're willing to take to get there?

Chapter 27

Rebel Rising Within

I started my new job with hope, but it wasn't the beginning I had imagined.

There was no real onboarding. A few forms. A quick thirty-minute overview of their order-entry system. And that was it. I was also surprised to learn that one of the direct reports they had promised to wait to hire until I started was already in place.

Almost immediately, I noticed a pattern.

Every recommendation I made was met with resistance. Every idea had to be justified, defended, and broken down to the smallest detail. Nothing moved without pushback.

I had been transparent when they hired me. I told them about my PTSD. I told them what I had survived. I did that so they would understand my needs, and so they would be prepared in the unlikely event that Damon ever showed up.

Instead, the constant back-and-forth with my boss and the agency's principals began to wear on me.

That October, my grandmother passed away.

She was the one who owned the hotel.

The one I inherited my entrepreneurial spirit.

I had just started my workday when I got the call. I was devastated.

The agency offered three days of bereavement leave. Her funeral was out of town, so I planned to keep working until I needed the days for travel. Fridays were half days, and my team always left before me. That Friday, just two days after my grandmother passed, I was placed into a meeting for a funeral home account.

I couldn't believe the insensitivity.

It wasn't even a guaranteed project. When I expressed my discomfort, the project manager apologized and then asked, "Why couldn't someone from your team be here?" forgetting that they had already left for the day.

A few months later, the agency changed its policy. From that point on, employees had to use personal vacation time to attend a family member's funeral.

I barely recognized the place anymore.

The environment continued to deteriorate. My team began quietly searching for new jobs. I did too. Then the agency terminated a sweet woman going through a divorce with an infant at home. She had done nothing to warrant it.

The toxicity was undeniable.

Not long after, my marketing manager gave her two-week notice. I wasn't surprised. During her exit meeting, a client video was shown for my approval. It was an online video with a massive QR code in the center. It made no sense. Online videos are clickable. A QR code that large was unnecessary.

I said so.

My boss exploded.

He began arguing with me in front of the team.

I removed myself and went back to my office.

Moments later, he came charging in. Finger pointing. Words flying. He slammed the door shut behind him.

Immediately, I felt unsafe.

My body began to shake. His words blurred into noise. I tried to leave. He stepped in front of me. I moved. He blocked me again. The third time, I had had enough.

I shoved past him with my hip, opened the door, and said, "Get out. No one is going to make me feel unsafe in my own office."

I was shaking uncontrollably. I fled to the bathroom and began hyperventilating. A new employee came in and tried to comfort me. Then another. Then another.

I was in a full trigger. Flashbacks hit hard
and fast.

A project manager who served on the
board of a domestic violence
organization urged me to speak with the
CEO. I did.

He sat across from me, stoic and cold.

As I shared what happened, he said,
"That doesn't sound like the man I
know."

With one sentence, my credibility was
erased.

He told me to go home early.

When I got home, my mom was already
there. We were supposed to leave for
Nashville the next day for her birthday.
She took one look at me and knew
something was wrong. I told her
everything.

It felt like another assault.

Later that evening, I received a meeting
invite for the next morning at 8:30 a.m.
with the CEO and my boss.

I knew exactly what was coming.

They weren't going to take my voice.

I accepted the invitation.

Then I wrote two emails.

One was my resignation to leadership.

The other went to the entire agency. In it, I explained my resignation in my own words. I thanked my colleagues. I spoke honestly about my mental health and recent events. And I signed it the only way that felt right:

No one will ever take my voice.

I scheduled both emails to be sent at exactly 8:30 a.m. The time of our scheduled meeting.

Then I arrived at 9:00 to clean out my office. My mother came with me for support.

For an hour and a half, the CEO and the project manager stood outside my office door, watching.

I walked out knowing two things.

No one would ever make me feel small again.

And no one would ever take my voice again.

The Rebel had awakened.

Reflection

Rising Your Inner Rebel

There's a point when you stop trying to be understood by people who are committed to misunderstanding you. You stop negotiating your worth. You stop shrinking to keep the peace. You choose yourself, out loud, even if your voice shakes.

A Note to You

If you've been waiting for permission to speak up, this is it. Your voice counts. It always has.

Rebel Rising

What is one thing you are no longer available for, and what are you choosing instead?

Epilogue

After I left my job, I decided to start my own digital marketing agency, Media Rebel. From there came my podcast, Media Rebel Unplugged, which now ranks in the top 10 percent of podcasts worldwide in its first year. I also formed a second agency with business partners focused on destination marketing called Porchlyt.

I've been focused on growing my faith and walk with God and was baptized and made new in October of 2024. I give God all the glory that I am still standing here today. I often reflect on what made Damon stop hitting me that night. It was either realizing he was going to kill me or God Himself. I'd like to think it was God.

I launched my website, janicebeckerofficial.com, to focus on

keynote speaking and the Rebel Rising
Retreat, which will be held in October
2026 and every year after.

I plan to write a second book that will
explore this next chapter of my journey.
I look forward to sharing it when the
time feels right.

My hope is that somewhere in these
pages, you found moments that
resonated with you. Moments that
helped you recognize the Rebel Within
yourself. She is there. She always has
been.

Embrace her.

I wish you many blessings and love.

Janice Becker

Stay Connected

To learn more about Janice, or to book her for a speaking engagement, visit janicebeckerofficial.com.

If you're interested in attending a Rebel Rising retreat, visit rebelrisingretreat.com.

You can also find all of Janice's social links on her website if you'd like to follow along.

Janice plans on writing her second book, which continues the story after she left her job.

About The Author

Janice M. Becker is a domestic violence survivor, CEO, keynote speaker, podcaster and author. Her work is grounded in lived experience and focused on helping women reconnect with their voice, rebuild self-trust, and choose what comes next with clarity and purpose.

She is the CEO of marketing agencies Porchlyt and Media Rebel, and the host of the Media Rebel Unplugged podcast, where she shares real conversations around leadership, resilience, and growth.

In 2024, Janice was nominated as a Northeast Ohio Smart Woman in the Progressive Woman category and is a member of the American Marketing Association.

Janice lives and works in Northeast Ohio and continues to write, speak, and encourage women who are ready to rise despite what life has challenged them with.